Duffer's Debut

An Introduction to Golf
Its Culture, Customs & Conventions

by
Ted Ronberg

illustrated by Kieron O'Gorman

Canadian Cataloguing in Publishing Data

Ronberg, Ted, 1941

    Duffer's debut: an introduction to golf
    its culture, customs & conventions

Includes index.
ISBN 0-9684551-0-7
    1. Golf. I. Title.

GV965.R64 1999   796.352   C98-901318-9

Published by: Morin, Ronberg & Associates Inc.
Orleans P.O. Box 462, Ottawa, Ontario, Canada

Printed by: Tri-Co Printing
To order visit out website at "http://www.duffersdebut.com".

Illustrations by Kieron O'Gorman
Edited by Jenny Strickland

Table of Contents

Dedication.. ix

Introduction xi

Part A
Understanding Golf

Chapter 1:
The Environment 3

What is golf? 3

Who plays golf? 3

Where is golf played? 5

When is golf played? 6

Why play golf? 7

Chapter 2:
Golf: The Game.. 9

The Objective 9

Handicaps... 10

Rules 11

The playing field 13

First, the Tee 13

Second, the Fairway 13

Third, the Green 14

Equipment 15

The Ball 15

The Tee 16

The Clubs 17

Chapter 3:
Off-Course golf **19**

Television 19

Magazines and Books 20

Computer games 21

Indoor Driving Ranges 21

Home Putting Greens 22

Part B
Getting Ready to Play

Chapter 4:
Getting started **25**

The Initiation 25

Buying Equipment 26

Lessons 31

    Golf School 33

    Golf Course Pro Shop 33

    Driving Range 33

    Winter Golf School / Night School Courses 34

A Place to play 35

People to Play with 37

Expectations 39

Pre-Season Fitness 42

Chapter 5:
Preparing to play **43**

Choosing the Tee-off Time 43

Using Power Carts 45

Dress Code 47

Sign-in at the pro shop 48

Last minute checks 49

    The Golfer 49

    The Equipment 49

Stretching 50

Pre-game practice 51

Part C
Your Debut - First Time on the Course

Chapter 6:
    Scene I - The Tee 57

Chapter 7:
    Scene II -The Fairway 61

Chapter 8:
    Scene III -The Approach 67

Chapter 9:
    Scene IV - The Green 71

Chapter 10:
    Managing the Round 75

Chapter 11:
    The 19th Hole 79

Part D
Duffer's Do's

Checklists for Beginners 83

    A. Learning the game 83

    B. Being ready to play 84

    C. Playing safely 85

    D. Efficient golf 87

    E. Course Etiquette 89

    F. Low Stress golf 90

    G. Care of the Course 92

    H. Profile of an Ideal Beginner 93

Part E
Epilogue & References

Epilogue 97

Glossary of Golfing Terms 99

Index 109

List of Illustrations

Dudley in his debut ....Cover
Dudley 4
Dolly.. 4
At the cross-roads 5
Waking up to play 7
The objective of golf 9
New and experienced golf balls 15
The Tee 16
The Clubs.. 17
Ball trajectories for various clubs 18
The couch duffer 19
Getting started 25
Buying equipment 27
Taking lessons 32
Enjoying winter golf.. 34
People to play with 37
Expectations 40
Choosing the tee-off time 43
Walking vs. Carting 46
Dress code 47
Stretching 51
The Tee 57
The Fairway 61
Hazard in the hazard.. 63
The Approach bunker... 67
The Green 71
Git Along li'l Duffer 75
The 19th Hole... 79
Learning the game 83
Ready to play 84
Playing safely 86
Efficient golf.. 87
Course etiquette... 89
Low stress golf 91
Care of the course 92
The ideal beginner 94

Dedication

This book is dedicated to all the saints who have humoured, advised and indulged me as I sweated through the seemingly interminable stages of learning the game of golf. I have been continually astounded by their patience, tolerance and understanding. These include my late father, Bill Ronberg, who bought me my first set of clubs when I graduated from high school and, despite overwhelming evidence to the contrary, never gave up hope that I might one day become a mediocre player. Heartfelt thanks go to my wife Ann who, while encouraging me to improve my game, has never failed to express her amazement that someone with so little natural talent could persist in what seemed to be an essentially fruitless exercise. I also appreciate the contribution of my mother Roma who, is in her ninth decade and slightly more than 5'-1" and 100 pounds. She has maintained my sense of humility by seldom allowing her motherly instincts extend to allowing her first-born to outscore her over 9 holes. Finally, thanks to my two sons, Rick and Rob, whose youthful prowess has given me the motivation to progress from duffer to golfer.

This book is <u>not</u> dedicated to the wags who, when approached for suggestions on improving my golf, offered that my problem is club selection - I should have joined a book club.

This book would not have been possible without the invaluable contributions of the following devotees of golf: first, my numerous instructors who have anguished over the small return for their considerable investment of time, including Marc Peterson, Director of the Golf School at the Ottawa Athletic Club and Mike Plunkett, assistant Professional at Camelot Golf and Country Club. Second, those seasoned golfers and fellow club members who have helped me to learn, understand and appreciate the many aspects of golf (including Phil Cleary, Bob Mercer, Hugh O'Gorman, Al Clayton and Ross Couchman). I particularly want to acknowledge Bob Durant, Sportscaster and host of the popular golf show "The Golf Report" heard on CFRB in Toronto, and the numerous beginners, aspiring golfers and fellow duffers (including John MacNeill, Nancy Kenny, Tim Larock, Jean Morin and Anne Leger) and those friends and fellow travellers, past and present, who have indulged my flailings and wailings, often to the detriment of their own game. I am also indebted to Robin Stafford, the Course Superintendent at Camelot, who has helped me appreciate that a golf course is much more than just a really big front lawn.

Ted Ronberg
19 September, 2000

Introduction

I am a middle-aged civil engineer and business consultant who decided five years ago, after selling the family country cottage, to take up golf. Up to that point I had played three to five times a year, mostly in office tournaments, but had never taken a lesson. The objective then, had been merely to enjoy the company of friends and colleagues whose aptitude and talent were about as abysmal as mine but who nevertheless enjoyed any excuse to escape the office scene for five hours of fresh air and sunshine. Humour and good-natured teasing set the tone for the day. Competence was not an issue and few had any interest in learning, let alone mastering the game. The prevailing viewpoint was that good golfers were the idle rich, retired people or insurance salesmen. Normal folk balancing family and professional commitments didn't have the time to master golf's intricacies.

Two events galvanized me into taking a hard second look at golf. First, my two teenage sons enrolled in a junior golf school at a local course and proved, beyond a shadow of a doubt, that either they possessed athletic genes which had undoubtedly skipped my generation or, alternatively, that my sons and I were not related . This sobering realization, together with an infusion of spare time arising from the sale of the cottage, created an opportunity for me to better my hand at that finest of Scottish pastimes.

Having tried unsuccessfully to learn the game by practising at driving ranges, taking a few lessons, and touring the many local courses, I became frustrated by my lack of progress. Then, five years ago, driven by an overwhelming sense of athletic desperation, I took out a membership at a new golf club only 15 minutes from home. I remain a chronic duffer to this very day who aspires, in the future, to play consistently below 100. My experiences are the foundation for this book.

I have directed this book at aspiring golfers in the process of taking up or intending to take up the great game of golf. Its purpose is to acquaint the beginner with the culture, customs and conventions of the game so as to better understand it and to make venturing out onto the course more comfortable. It does not cover technique, (there are already countless books on that subject!) but rather, is an aid to appreciating and enjoying the game. You will find no prescription here for a correct swing (this is best learned from qualified instructors) but you should gain some insight into the thought processes that typically occur as a golfer approaches, and progresses through, a round of golf. It is said by many professionals that golf is largely a mental game. In learning to play, I have come to realize that the cerebral aspect of golf pertains not only to the tactics and strategy associated with placing shots and reading greens, but to the concentration and focus required to set up and execute any successful shot. Unlike many sports that are largely reactive in nature, golf is essentially pro-active.

My real purpose in writing this book is to document for the benefit of newcomers, (and while the experience is still fresh in my mind), the important non-physical aspects of the game and the journey to be travelled while evolving from a duffer into a golfer.

I make no absolute guarantees about the reliability or accuracy of information presented here, but I can confirm that the text has been vetted by professionals and seasoned golfers, and by a random selection of current learners or beginners whom I judged to share my athletic dysfunctionality. My ideas have been gleaned not only from personal experiences but from my interaction with those I have encountered along the road, including pros, fellow novices, players of every stripe and level of ability and friends. My hope is that, by sharing this information, beginners will grasp more readily the essence of golf and enjoy it from the first swing. Golf is a challenge to learn but infinitely rewarding!

To seasoned golfers browsing through this text, I would like to remind you that, having just recently "been through the mill", my observations and experiences are intended to reflect how the game is seen by those learning it and how you and other experienced players are presenting the game to newcomers.

This book is organized to conform to the normal path to be followed by any beginner from buying equipment, through taking lessons to playing the first rounds from tee to green and from the first to the last hole. Part D - Duffer's Do's (Checklists for Beginners) summarizes the key points made in the book, including the profile of an ideal beginner from the perspective of other golfers.

Part A

Understanding Golf

Chapter 1:
The Environment

What is golf?

Golf is a good walk with a mission. It is both a sport and a leisure pastime. Golf is also pleasure, fresh air, exercise, a sense of escape or exhilaration, but is equally capable of causing frustration, tears, marital problems and family breakdown. Depending on the day, golf may seem to be either a vengeful or brilliant contrivance of mediaeval Scots. In short, it is the total experience including conversation, humour, unwinding, competition, open rivalry and ruthless wagering. A given round can be a meeting, an interview, a sales call or a bonding session. As a sport it is unique, in that the opponents include yourself and the field of play as well as the other players. It is, sometimes, overwhelmingly, a game of rules, but it is also a game of honour where players are their own referees and routinely award themselves penalties. Golf can also become a passion or (at worst) an obsession. Few people exposed to it have remained indifferent. Reactions range from contempt to addiction. Unlike most pro sports, there are few spectators or fans who have not played it at one time.

Who plays golf?

Golf can be played by men, women and children of any age and build. They come tall or short, light or heavy, strong or weak, fast or slow, for richer or for poorer, smart or not so smart and (most importantly!) athletic or non-athletic. Among sports enthusiasts it is considered the great equalizer.

Despite the wide range of those able to play the game, golf also has its stereotypes. The common perception of the typical golfer as well-off, middle-aged and overweight is not too far off the mark. Personal experience allows me to report that I have also found golfers (with notable exceptions) to share the following common characteristics:

- friendly and warm with a good sense of humour

- polite with good social graces

- well spoken and informed

- intelligent and alert

- honest and open

- patient and understanding

- continuously learning the game

After randomly listing these attributes, I was struck by their positive character and by their resemblance to the requirements of a new career ad or the wish list for the ideal soul-mate. Nevertheless, I am convinced that they portray a reasonably accurate picture of the typical golfer as a generally mature, well-adjusted, good-natured, and just plain nice person. So one of the great pleasures of the game is the opportunity to associate with interesting, first rate people - the gentlefolk who play golf.

Where is golf played?

Golf is enjoyed (or suffered) on a dedicated playing ground known as a golf course: a plot of land generally occupying about 150 to 200 acres of former farmland, forest, waterway, seashore or desert. The course may include housing bordering the fairways - confirmation that a benevolent developer has rescued a previously unproductive environmental wasteland by converting it into prime real estate. Each course consists of 9 or 18 holes, each having several tees, a fairway with hazards, and a green. Each course also usually offers a clubhouse containing a pro shop, a restaurant and bar, and locker rooms. Next to the clubhouse you invariably find a practice putting green and often, a driving range. Most golf courses are located in the urban fringe but they are increasingly being constructed in vacation resorts, at times totally removed from an urban setting. Some vacation areas (such as Myrtle Beach, South Carolina) focus primarily on golf, and have more courses than major cities.

Golf courses vary greatly in design and topography. They may be of the open grassland/seaside (links) variety, or forested (parkland). Fairways may be narrow or wide, flat or hilly and they commonly embrace wet and dry hazards: sandtraps (bunkers) or water.

All courses are cleverly designed to disguise their true difficulty and to lure the unsuspecting amateur into a false sense of security on approaching their lair of impending tragedies.

A typical 18 hole course is 5,000 to 7,000 yards long (some courses are metric) in total direct playing distance from tee to green, and requires the player to cover about 5 miles to complete the game from the 1st tee to the 18th green. Generally, golf courses occupy prime land with picturesque to spectacular landscapes resulting in the game being kind to the senses if potentially cruel to the psyche.

As with all things, golf courses range in quality and cost, from the budget ($15 to $20 per round) informal public course with modest facilities, to the expensive ($150 to $200 per round) prestigious and impeccably groomed resort course with all the posh amenities. Such variety provides options for all tastes and pocketbooks, making it easy for anyone to find a place where they can play comfortably.

When is golf played?

In our neck of the woods, golf is played in the months of May through October with some courses opening early in April and remaining open through November, the termination of play dictated by ambient temperature or snow cover. Golf is played in the daylight hours from opening time until dusk, with the first starting time determined by the time required after daybreak to cut the first fairways, tees and greens. Many courses have a set opening time that is adjusted to the nearest half hour, depending on sunrise. Courses are sometimes closed due to rainfall, frost (to avoid damage to the turf) or fog (to avoid damage to golfers) and are usually closed when electrical storms threaten. Most responsible greens keepers will not permit morning play before cutting is completed on the first holes, or after the course is officially closed for the season.

Why play golf?

The principal reasons for playing golf are:

1. The fresh air (unless the course is downwind from the garbage dump)

2. The exercise (an 18 hole round is a five mile walk)

3. That sense of escape (you'll forget <u>all</u> your other problems)

4. Stress management (it's a different kind of stress!)

5. Fellowship (three players share or ridicule your misery)

6. Sheer enjoyment of the game (like radiation, it increases with exposure)

7. Relaxation (you'll be really relaxed - <u>after</u> the round)

8. It's food for the soul (courses have a natural, pleasant setting)

9. The personal challenge (you compete at every turn against yourself, the course and other players)

10. Business development (how else can you book a five hour client meeting?)

As an enthusiastic beginner, you should have at least the first five reasons on your list. Understand, of course, that golf, like marriage, has its inevitable quota of bad days. Even then, when nothing seems to go right, you can console yourself by falling back on fresh air and exercise as your justification for playing the game.

Chapter 2:
Golf: The Game

The Objective

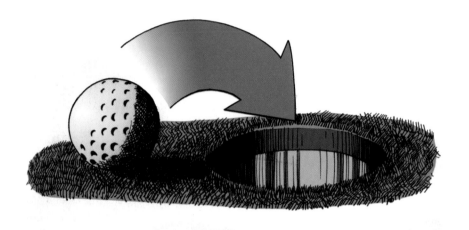

The goal of golf - the game is, using clubs, to propel a small (and usually reluctant!) white ball from the starting line (the "tee") along a stretch of fairway into a small round hole on the green, using as few strokes as possible. This process is repeated for each hole on the course until all 18 (or 9 for a half course) holes are completed. Ideally, each hole is played in the same low number of strokes required by an accomplished golfer. This "ideal" score is known as PAR and varies for each hole depending on its length and difficulty. For the typical par 4 hole the par golfer will use one stroke to drive off from the tee, a second stroke to hit the ball from the fairway onto the green, and finally two strokes on the green using a putter to roll the ball into the hole. Most holes are par 4's but for variety, each course also has short holes, judged to be par 3's and longer holes played as par 5's. It is extremely difficult (for a beginner make that impossible) to score par on every hole during a round of 18 holes. Even the pros seldom accomplish this feat and there is a tremendous gulf between the abilities of an accomplished golfer and a beginner!

Handicaps

Golf is one of the few sports where recreational players of such varying abilities can actually compete realistically. This balance is achieved by the classification of golfers' abilities using a handicap system. Handicaps vary from 0 to 40 for women and 0 to 36 for men with pros having a 0 (scratch) or lower handicap (e.g. +8) leaving the beginners at the opposite end of the scale. A handicap is calculated as the difference between the course rating and a golfer's average score for 18 holes. It is based on the best 10 of a golfer's last 20 games. When this handicap is subtracted from a player's gross (actual) score, the resulting net score can then be used as the basis for comparison. Therefore, a 20 handicapper playing one of his/her typical games will need an average of 92 strokes to play a par 72 course; however, if this same player were to shoot a 91, the net score of 71 (91-20) would beat the net score of a scratch handicapper shooting a 72 (72-0). You know that you've landed in the middle of a pro game if the players are competing on a gross rather than net score basis with no acknowledgment for their handicaps.

In addition to handicaps for players, there is a "slope" system for golf courses whereby all courses are assigned a slope rating (e.g. 115) that indicates their difficulty relative to a baseline standard course rated at 100. (Skiing also uses slopes, and like skiing you will frequently feel that your golf is downhill most of the time.) This takes into account the difficulty of each course played and, using these course slope ratings, allows regular golfers to be assigned a "handicap index". This system means that a score of 100 on a difficult course is considered to be better than the same score on an easy course.

As a beginner, you will inevitably be considered a "high handicapper" by other golfers. When someone asks "What's your handicap?", the safest response for some time will, just as inevitably be, "Myself."

Rules

There are only <u>two</u> key rules in golf:

- Play the ball where it lies. (except when the Rules of Golf allow moving it); and

- Count every stroke.

However, such basic rules only serve the golfer who remains on the fairway and doesn't get into trouble, a situation that almost never occurs. Trouble invariably comes in one or more of the following ways:

- you lose your ball (usually in long grass or the bush)

- you hit your ball into a pond or creek (marked by red or yellow stakes)

- your ball is unplayable because it's:
  - embedded in the ground
  - too near a rock or tree
  - under the lip of a sand trap, or
  - there's no room for a backswing

- your ball lands on the fairway in water or in ground under repair

- your ball lands on a cartpath

- your ball lands out of bounds - i.e. off the golf course property and usually marked by white stakes

- you play the wrong ball

- you completely miss the ball on your swing

- you hit your ball twice on the same swing

- you hit yourself with the ball (yes, dear Duffers, it really <u>can</u> happen)

- an animal takes off with your ball (usually a fox employed by the pro)

- you hit another ball while putting (guaranteed to not endear you to the other player)

These are but a few of the common challenges encountered during a typical game. There are many others. Golf is a game of rules which, for beginners, are overwhelmingly complicated and perplexing. To help you through this bureaucratic maze and to ensure that everyone plays the game the same way and with no advantage, the golf gurus have developed the ultimate rule book. This book is known as (you guessed it!) <u>The Rules of Golf</u> and is produced jointly by The Royal and Ancient Golf Club of St. Andrews, Scotland and The United States Golf Association. The book is available from your local golf shop or pro shop. Every beginner should encourage a golfing friend to buy or borrow a copy. This friend can then explain them to you to help you acquire a sense of the game so you know how to proceed or where to refer when you run into strange or unusual situations.

For beginners, an in-depth knowledge of the rules is far from imperative. You won't be playing competitive golf for some time, maybe never, and will only need to know the basics. Knowing the rules can save you strokes, but you can easily pick them up by osmosis as you play or by discussing new situations with the other players. Don't be misled by those who consider the rules arcane, silly and too complex. Once you take the time to learn them, you will find that they are straightforward and practical and make the game fair for all players.

The playing field

The foremost challenge in golf comes from the terrain or playing field, which varies not only from course to course but also from hole to hole, and from tee to green on the same hole. A golf course is a living setting whose conditions are constantly altered by rain, wind, temperature and lighting. Adapting to changing conditions and planning one's route to the hole is known in golf as "course management", aptly named, because no course I know of presents fewer hazards than those encountered on a typical day at the office. Each of the three parts of every hole - tee, fairway and green represents unique challenges requiring distinctive approaches, techniques and skills. The salient characteristics of these geographic golf features are as follows:

First, the Tee

Each tee should provide the golfer with a good view of the ultimate goal, the hole, before teeing off and for this reason is usually elevated above the succeeding fairway. A yardage marker indicates the distance from each set of tee blocks (traditionally red for ladies or white for men) to the centre of the green. These distances are measured from the mid position of the blocks (they are moved every morning to reduce wear) and therefore are seldom exact. For beginners, however, they are accurate enough to help you chose a club from your bag for teeing off. From the tee you can usually see all the hazards on or adjacent to the fairway but this may be of limited value as you will also have difficulty in estimating the real impact of the tee's elevation on your shot. For those who flunked high school physics, a tee higher than the fairway gives a longer than average shot whereas a tee facing an ascending fairway shortens the shot.

Second, the Fairway

This is where most of the real action takes place on a golf course. Tee shots and putting present obvious challenges, while fairways are both a physical and mental minefield. Sandtraps, water hazards and "the rough" are conspicuous obstacles, but there are additional insidious difficulties:

- downhill or uphill lies *

- sidehill lies, either above or below you

- lies where your view of the green is blocked

- lies blocked by trees, where you have to go over or around the tree

- lies on cartpaths or ground under repair, where you may move your ball without penalty

- sharply angled fairways (called dog's legs) where you are obliged to either fly the angle or bend your shot around it.

- divot marks that make shots from this depressed lie more difficult

* N.B. A downhill lie may also be a tale whose believability decreases with the telling . An uphill lie is the opposite. When successfully told, this prevarication may be accepted as fact. Sidehill lies lead nowhere.

Third, the Green

The finale for each hole takes place on the green. Here a beginner can play with even the most accomplished players as putting is considerably less difficult than a regular golf swing. Consider that only one club is used, the putter, and the terrain is relatively tame compared to the fairway. Greens have only two variables : speed and slope. If the greens are judged to be "fast" the ball will roll farther than usual for a given stroke weight. Sloped greens are a particular challenge as they are designed to make it difficult to judge the "break" or distance a ball will roll either to the left or right of a straight line between the ball position and the hole. The slope also presents a further and equally diabolical enigma requiring you to estimate the direction and distance that a ball will roll uphill or downhill compared to a flat lie.

Equipment

Despite the plethora of modern golf accessories, there are really only three essential items of golf equipment - the ball, the tee, and the clubs.

'Before'

'After'

The Ball

This is the small white projectile that you try to launch into inner space from each tee. The ball is a 1-3/4" diameter attractively dimpled sphere (dimples reduce air friction and cause it to fly farther) with an elastic core and a tough synthetic outer cover. When struck cleanly by a clubface held perpendicular to the path of the swing, it can travel anywhere from 100 to 300 yards straight down any given fairway. However, this distance is reduced when the ball is hit with an open (the toe or end of the clubface points slightly backwards) or closed-faced club both of which will impart a lateral spin to its flight. This spin produces a difference in air friction between the two sides of a flying ball causing it to curve either - away from the golfer (i.e. to the right for a right-handed golfer - a "fade" or a "slice") or - towards the golfer (i.e. to the left for a right-handed golfer - a "draw" or a "hook"). Both directions of spin significantly reduce the distance of the shot.

The Tee

This is the short wooden peg used to raise your ball off the turf when teeing off in order to produce a clear striking path between the club and the ball. This means there will be no grass in the way of the club. The tee also comes in handy for cleaning the grooves on clubfaces, temporarily marking a ball placement if you've lost your ball marker and for repairing ballmarks on the green when you forget your pitchfork.

The Clubs

D 5W 3W 3I 4I 5I 6I 7I 8I 9I PW SW Putter

figure 1: A typical selection of golf clubs

The rules of golf permit the golfer to carry up to 14 clubs in the golf bag making for a generally heavy ensemble. The selection usually includes a driver, a 3 wood, a 5 wood, 7 irons numbered 3 to 9, a pitching wedge, a sand wedge and a putter (for a total of 13, see *figure 1* above), plus one additional club to cater to the special needs of the individual golfer (often a 7 wood or lob wedge). Each club has distinctive and varying features including the length and stiffness of the shaft, and the slope (or "loft"), lie, shape and material of the club head. With a swing uniform in terms of speed and form, club selection alone may determine the distance and trajectory of a ball's flight. The distance of each shot is a direct function of the speed and the angle of the striking clubface. Even though the swing speed may be

PW

8I

6I

3W

D

figure 2: Ball trajectories for various clubs.

constant, the speed of the clubface is determined by the length of the shaft. So, the clubface speed of a driver is much faster than that of a pitching wedge since it travels through a longer swing arc in the same period of time. A shaft that is 20% longer produces considerably more than a 20% increase in club head speed and a proportional increase in the distance travelled by the ball. Complicating this complex relationship is the fact that as the club length increases, the loft of the club decreases. This means that a driver gives the ball a flatter, longer trajectory with a longer roll than a pitching wedge which hits the ball high and lands it with a comparatively shorter roll (see *figure 2* above). The club numbering system assigns the highest number to the club having the greatest loft or the one whose clubface slopes back at the greatest angle from vertical. Remember : high number = high (and short!) trajectory. It is particularly noteworthy for beginners that the shorter clubs give greater control over the ball flight than the longer clubs.

Chapter 3:
Off-Course golf

One of the great pleasures of golf is to be found in pre-season fantasies about the awesome games yet to be played on legendary courses in the upcoming season. Depending on the zeal of the particular golfer, this escape may take hold in the first week of the off-season. Really committed golfers also manage to hone their obsession through a variety of related off-course activities. These may prove helpful in that they complement the physical aspects of the game while providing insight into the psychology of more experienced golfers.

Television

There are PGA and LPGA tournaments on television virtually every weekend. Watching them is not only highly instructive as to the techniques and level of course management required to play intelligent golf, but is also highly entertaining. Pros constantly pull off next-to-impossible shots, with startling displays of eagles, birdies and holes-in-one, while occasionally reminding viewers of their humanity and essential vulnerability by masterfully duffing a shot into the water or bush. This drama is often highlighted by running commentary from former professional golfers, who cannot resist trying to get inside the mind of each golfer to analyse or second guess the thought process leading up to each shot. With up to $100,000 or more riding on a single shot, the pros' reactions and the human dimension of play can be captivating. This spectacle gives the beginner a solid appreciation of the challenges integral to golf, regardless of ability and helps to bond all players into the community of golfers. Also, perhaps sadistically, there is nothing better for the beginner's ego than watching a pro duff a shot producing a result little better than that of a typical 40 handicapper.

In addition to the weekend tournaments there are numerous golf shows on television, many of which focus on teaching the fundamentals of the game.

Magazines and Books

Magazines provide a continuous flow of information on the latest equipment, techniques, and golfing events. They also offer interesting personality sketches of the tour golfers. The advantage of magazines, of course, is that they can be enjoyed and reread in leisurely moments when you're in a golf mood. Unlike TV, there is also ample time to, at your leisure, digest the points being made. Both the major magazines, *Golf Digest* and *Golf* are well illustrated with colour photos and diagrams and are a real pleasure to read. To beginners, I would recommend being a regular subscriber, in the first few years anyway.

There are countless books on the technical aspects of golf, but few convey a real sense of the game, let alone its traditions and culture. The best book that I have read about golf is Lorne Rubenstein's masterpiece *Links*.

Computer games

Video games are usually based on particularly famous courses and allow players to experience the individual holes. They respect the mental dimension of golf and give beginners a feel for the terminology and psychology of the game. If you enjoy this medium, these games are a lot of fun. My chief lament is that they don't include a profile of the player's actual abilities i.e. slice every drive 20 yards to the right. On the other hand, maybe experiencing the fantasy of performing well, even when mother nature hasn't supplied natural ability, isn't such a bad thing.

Indoor Driving Ranges

These are a relatively recent development. When the links sap begins to course through a golfer's veins in late winter/early spring, nothing is better, both physically and psychologically, than hitting a bucket of balls to prepare for the coming season. There are two main kinds of indoor ranges: those where you can hit a regular shot either into a net or up to 80 yards under an inflated dome, and those where you hit a ball into a net with a computerized graphic of a fairway on a screen behind the net. The former is like hitting on a regular outdoor range except distances are shorter, the drawback being that if you have a bad slice or hook, you miss the later, worst part of the shot. (Now I understand why they're so popular!) On the computerized ranges there is an automated tee that reads the speed and orientation of your club and creates a visual image of the ball as you have actually hit it. Although such feedback is hard on the ego, the graphics generated give reasonably accurate feedback on how you are actually hitting the ball. While they are an excellent motivation for improving what may be a somewhat dismal game they do little to impress anyone who might be watching with a view to cheering your efforts.

Home Putting Greens

Y ou are probably unaware that you are already the proud owner
of an excellent green where your putting skills can be honed in
the off season. Known commonly as the living room carpet, this practice green usually has a slope and texture closely resembling a typical green. Using a glass, Aunt Martha's vase, or any of the myriad
putting targets available from golf stores, you can spend countless
happy hours perfecting your short and medium putts, all in the comfort of home and close to the source of your favourite home brew.

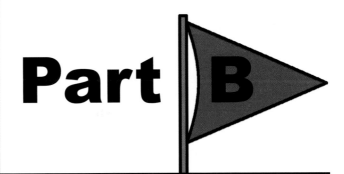

Part B

Getting Ready
to Play

Chapter 4:
Getting started

The Initiation

For a raw recruit in the army of golf beginners, attitude is every thing! Therefore, when you begin by playing military golf (left, right, left, right down the fairway) recognize that golf (next to marriage of course) can be life's most infuriatingly frustrating and intimidating experience. Granted, the journey should now be easier given that you now have the benefit of the priceless wisdom being divulged in this text. Nevertheless, it is important to recognize that getting started on the right foot with a positive mindset requires the humility of a rookie, a brain like a sponge and the eagerness of a bridegroom.

If you have never played golf but think that you would enjoy the game, the place to begin is on a driving range. Get a golfer friend or the range pro to show you the basics in technique — the grip, the stance and the swing — and then proceed to hack your way through a small basket of balls with a 7 iron. To make the ball easier to hit, ensure you place it on a tee . Once you discover that this is an exercise in total frustration and that you are, unfortunately, not a "natural" (which puts you in a league with 99.9 percent of all beginners), your next step should be lessons. What you will have undoubtedly gleaned from this painful initiation, (perhaps by observing some energetic youngsters flailing alongside you) is that a successful golf swing has absolutely nothing in common with swinging a baseball bat or an axe. Whatever your degree of success with this first experience, <u>do not</u>, I repeat, <u>do not</u> book a tee-off time. You are not ready to venture out onto a golf course until you are able to hit 75% of your shots at least 100 yards and no more than 25 to 30 yards off-line. Until this happy moment arrives, you are confined to golf lessons and the driving range. When you can easily pass this self test, you can then book your first tee-off time knowing that you are capable of spending most of the day on the fairway without the fear of unduly embarrassing yourself or injuring fellow players.

Buying Equipment

One dilemma for golf beginners, as in other sports, is whether to buy "make-do" or quality equipment. My recommendation is that, having confirmed that you like the game, you should go the "make-do" route. This does not necessarily mean you have to use that fine hickory-shafted set inherited from great-uncle Harry. You could buy an inexpensive new or second-hand set (or half-set if the budget is tight) from a golf store or pro-shop. Golf is a highly individual sport and clubs that may be perfect for your good buddy Al may be exactly the wrong kind for you. Even the "greenest" golf shop sales attendant will help you make a better decision than you could on your own. When shopping for golf equipment, try to find someone knowledgeable, personable, patient and experienced who can help identify your needs. Depending on your level of commitment and interest in the game, you have the following shopping options:

- **A golf course pro shop**. This generally provides service and equipment well suited to beginners' needs. In a pro shop the salesperson is generally a teaching professional familiar with the problems of new golfers. As a bonus you also have the option of trying out new clubs at the course driving range. You may pay slightly more here but you really get value for money. Be sure to ask the pro if any members have suitable used clubs for sale. These could be a great bargain.

- **A golf store**. Here you will have a greater selection of equipment and a wider price range than at the pro shop and will get individual attention from salespeople. Some stores also carry used clubs. They should have a practice net where you can try out the clubs to see how they feel. Unless your liability insurance has a high limit, avoid practice swings in the aisle.

- **A sporting goods store**. These offer apparent price advantages through volume purchases but, as they sell all types of sporting equipment, will generally have less selection in golf equipment and less specialized sales staff to assist the raw beginner. Once you are familiar with the game you can look for bargains here.

- **Custom made golf shop.** Here you are able to get no-name clubs similar to name brand models. They are made (or rather, assembled) to your individual needs and matched to each other. These shops tend to be patronized by seasoned golfers who are already knowledgeable about the full range of available clubs and other equipment.

- **Garage sales**. Unless you're into cast-offs or antiques, beginners should only shop at garage sales when accompanied by a seasoned golfer who keeps you on a tight leash and refuses to let you make any decision on your own.

- **Newspaper Ads**. There are frequently bargains to be had here, particularly from disgruntled duffers who just can't hack it any more. (True golfers never retire.) When checking out these "bargains" be sure to bring along your seasoned golfer consultant.

After shopping for the basics, you should be the proud possessor of the following equipment:

- **Comfortable golf shoes**. An inexpensive pair may vary in price from $50 to $100, depending on make and style, and you will pay considerably more for the waterproof variety. My guess is that, as a beginning golfer, you may not be much into wet golf. Regular dry weather shoes should suffice. If you tend to be extremely cautious, buy the kind with the rubber-nubbed soles (i.e., without the individual spikes). These can then also be used as walking shoes should you find you golf less often than forecast. Since many courses are beginning to outlaw metal golf spikes, you should consider ordering the "soft" plastic spikes when buying regular golf shoes. Soft spikes are also more comfortable for walking. Unless you're actually looking for possible excuses to pack in a given game before completing 18 holes, remember that you'll be walking a full five miles and that uncomfortable shoes will add immeasurably to your frustration during a bad round.

- **A set of cavity-backed / perimeter-weighted irons (#3 to #9), 3 metal woods (#1,#3 and #5), a pitching wedge, a sand wedge, and a putter.** This is a full set. You may prefer a half set which foregoes the even-numbered irons. Some beginners, giving themselves every advantage, start their irons at number 5 and carry #5, #7 and #9 woods. These lofted clubs are considerably easier for beginners to use. Try to buy equipment that is no more than ten years old as older clubs will undoubtedly have smaller solid hitting areas on the club face (sweet spots) and therefore be harder to use. As the terms imply, cavity-backed / perimeter-weighted irons should be hollow on the back with the bulk of the clubhead weight concentrated at the perimeter of the clubface. To carry your clubs and all the other required paraphernalia, it is a tremendous advantage to have a golf bag with lots of pockets. You will find these handy to carry sandwiches and purely medicinal libations.

- **Golf balls**. Any kind of ball will do to start as long as they're not cut and haven't been submerged in water for too long. Old balls (like old golfers) lose their elasticity. You'll lose a lot of balls to start with and should not get fussy about their quality until you break 100 regularly on 18 holes. If you have a choice, try balls with a compression of 90, since they fly farther with a gentle swing. (You might even try an 80 if they're available.) All 100 compression balls are designed for a fast swing and usually are harder to hit. Happily, beginners find nearly as many balls as they lose since they spend a lot of quality time thrashing about in the bush or the water. If your supply of "foundlings" is huge and you're particularly perceptive, you'll discover that it is easier to putt consistently if you always use the same kind of ball - i.e. one that has the same compression and is made by the same manufacturer.

- **Clothing**. Almost all golf courses have a dress code where the tone is usually correct and conservative (see *Dress Code* in Chapter 5). This means wearing casual slacks, shorts (not too short!), or a skirt. Generally, men only wear skirts (i.e. kilts) on the course in Scotland. These are usually worn with a golf shirt having an open weave knit with short sleeves and a collar - important for freedom of movement, since a regular shirt, or blouse, will bind at the arms and waist when you attempt a full rotation swing. I find slacks practical for beginners who are often in the bush along with the mosquitoes, flies, burrs, nettles and poison ivy - unless, you're tough (or oblivious). In chosing colours for golf clothing, I tend to opt for the camouflage conservative shades that blend into the background. As a beginner you'll find that the quality of your golf will set you apart from other players as much as a hot pink golf shirt. Against changes in the weather, you'll also want to bring along a sweater and a waterproof jacket . It's a real revelation for beginners to experience how much the weather can change in four hours out on the course.

- **Golf glove**. Although not essential, this accessory will improve your grip on the clubs and protect your hand. It is worn on the hand nearest your target (left hand for a right-handed golfer).

- **Miscellaneous**. This category of equipment includes tees, ball markers, a pitch fork (for repairing ball marks on the greens), an umbrella, a ball retriever (not a large dog but a telescopic pole to assist your fellow players recover errant shots), sun screen, insect repellent, bandages, aspirins, food and any medication you might need over the duration of the round (anti-depressants could be helpful).

Remember the Boy Scout motto " Be Prepared ". If the foregoing list appears more suited to a Himalayan expedition than to a casual round of golf, keep in mind that a Mount Everest expedition is usually a once-in-a-lifetime event. With good luck and careful spousal management, you're hopefully going to be attacking the golf course two or three times a week.

Lessons

To successfully learn to play golf, lessons are the essential starting point. There are few people for whom the techniques and mechanics of the game are "natural". Hence, even for fast learners, instruction in the basics of the game is a prerequisite. Remember it can take years to change a bad habit once you've acquired one!

What are the options for someone wanting to learn the game? There are several, and fortunately, these available options allow an easy decision to be made in terms of quality of teaching and value for money. There appears to be a hierarchy in positions for golf pros with their ultimate goal to be the head pro at the semi-private/private clubs. However, since being a pro involves far more than teaching, the most senior or experienced pros are not necessarily the best teachers. Therefore, your options for instruction are:

Golf School

These schools offer the best in golf instruction. The focus of the school and the number-one job of its pros is to teach and advise students. These fully qualified teaching pros spend the bulk of their time giving lessons. Many are certified teaching professionals, some having taken a two-year college program in golf instruction. This is the best value for your money in that you get the best qualified and most experienced teachers.

Golf Course Pro Shop

Here the assistant pros usually do most of the teaching while the head pro manages the pro-shop including scheduling tee-off times and generally assisting players. You should watch out for any courses with small staffs where instruction may have a secondary role and receive less attention. Also avoid courses that have a substandard driving range or none at all.

If joining a club is in the back of your mind, you may wish to kill two birds with one stone by offering to take lessons while you check out and get the feel for the club and the course. Keep in mind however, that every course has its pros and cons.

Driving Range

To a beginning golfer it might appear that the preoccupation of driving ranges is to process golfers but their major advantage is that they have few competing responsibilities. This means that the range pro is more likely to have time to teach. Also, by taking lessons you become part of the range's mainstream business: that of hitting golf balls alongside other golfers. You pay for your balls as well as for the lessons. You should confirm whether the instructor is a certified teaching pro, although recently, some of the best teachers are working at quality driving ranges; these are often former head pros with equity in the range.

Winter Golf School / Night School Courses

This is a good way to be introduced to golf even if you're un-certain about your real level of interest in the game. Usually held in a local gym, these lessons will convey the basics of the game but without the atmosphere or feel of actual play on the golf course.

Here the pros may teach part time in the winter while their full-time compatriots are soaking up the sun in Florida or Arizona. The advantage of this setting is that there's not much golf being played in the north in January and anyhow, the gym is warm and never closed due to weather. You will also meet like-minded people who share your eagerness and challenges in learning the game.

A Place to play

Now let's assume that you have both your equipment and a few lessons under your belt to give you a feel for the game. Where then do you begin to play? The answer is - <u>not</u> on a golf course. As stated earlier, you start on a driving range and stay there until you can hit 75 to 80 percent of your shots at least 100 yards (with the club you intend to use off the tee - usually a driver), relatively straight: no more than 25 to 30 yards off centre. This does not mean that your shots have to be long or without a hook or slice but rather that you are able to place your shots with a fair degree of consistency (i.e. within the width of the average fairway). Such precautions save you the untold cost and trouble related to searching for lost balls while preventing you from hitting players in adjacent fairways once you venture out onto a "real" course. This approach saves you the cost of green fees and lost balls, time in driving to and from the course and time in walking the course, thereby avoiding untold frustration and humiliation but with just as much exercise. In this " no pressure" environment you will know intuitively when you are ready to graduate to the next level on a real golf course.

Once you have decided that you are ready for the "real thing", where do you begin?

Par 3 courses are the ideal starting point. You acquire the feeling of the game without being intimidated by long holes or major hazards. Because the holes are comparatively short, you will be using short, lofted irons. This means that your bad shots will not be that far off line relative to what they could be if you used woods or long irons. This in itself is a major confidence booster. If there is a choice of par 3 courses near you, opt for the "Executive par 3" variety which usually implies a course of higher quality (and price, unfortunately).

If you work for a large, progressive organization, you will un-doubtedly encounter the phenomenon of the "annual golf tourna-ment". This is a great opportunity for you to make an entrance into the wonderful world of golf. Here also, you may be certain that you will not be alone in demonstrating athletic ineptitude. You can rest assured that there will be many other duffers both less skilled and less embarrassed to show it. If you have begun the season at the driving range, you will be at your personal best by tournament time - usually late spring or early summer. If your company is among the socially enlightened, the format of the tournament will be a "scram-ble". This means that only the best shot among those made by each member of the foursome counts (which means that it probably won't be yours). Each player has the advantage of trying each shot from the tee or from where the "best ball" came to rest but not having to count it unless it is indeed the longest or best placed for the follow-ing shot. Since the seasoned "golfers" in your foursome will be go-ing for the home run on each shot, they will frequently "duff" it by hitting it into the bush or the water. This means that your modest effort has a greater chance of counting. If you really want to impress your team-mates, practice your putting before the tournament. This is where beginners usually excel. In any case, sign up for as many tournaments as you can. They are a lot of fun and are primarily so-cial rather than skill-oriented, so your play can be particularly dis-mal without anyone really noticing - and all the time you're learning.

With a few par three rounds or tournaments under your belt, you can now consider entering the field of honour on your own. Your best bet for easing into non-tournament golf on a regular course is to begin on a par three or relatively easy nine hole course. This means tackling a public course near your home, preferably one with a driv-ing range. I recommend driving around to check out what's avail-able, appealing and convenient before booking a tee-off time. The goal is to be comfortable with your choice since the plan is to return often. Then, having cajoled or coerced a buddy into joining your first venture, book a tee-off time and go for it!

People to Play with

G olf is a social sport. Bad golf with good people is unquestion-
ably better than good golf with irritating people. The ideal golf
partner is someone who is fun, easygoing and has a good sense of
humour. This partner should also be a person whose company you
enjoy and who plays at about the same level as you. This helps create
a sense of healthy competition while learning. You will find that you
learn faster when you can exchange observations and accomplish-
ments with a co-learner.

It's a definite advantage to have more than one partner as a
fellow learner and if you're really forward thinking you can strive
for as many as five. This arrangement will give you a full foursome
plus a spare when the happy day arrives that you're ready to tackle
your first rounds. Remember that as your golf improves, your circle
of potential golfing partners also grows. Better players will almost
always agree to play with beginners but tend to do so out of a sense
of public service. All golfers feel most comfortable when playing

with others of similar ability. Beginners should be constantly aware that they face a constant barrage of unsolicited, invaluable and overwhelming advice from more experienced golfers. Your duty as a beginner is to accept these well-meaning suggestions eagerly and gratefully, never for a moment displaying any doubt or concern about the value or sincerity of this selfless wisdom.

Special exceptions to all rules of reason and logic are required when you are called upon to play with your spouse. Then, you must possess the sensitivity, discretion, focus and consummate interpersonal skills of a diplomat. When exposed to the occasional frustrations of the game, normally mature adults, (and particularly those who golf only infrequently) suddenly display the patience-level of a pit bull, the vocabulary of a sailor and the emotional maturity of a two-year old. Do I have any advice for those courageous fools who dare to golf with their spouses? You bet! My list of cautions includes:

- Never try to teach your spouse. Let a pro take the abuse!

- Consider golf with your spouse as purely a social event. "Let's go out for a bite with the Joneses and that other couple tonight.... but hey it's such a nice evening, maybe we should play nine holes before dinner just to get to know each other ".

- Never plan on playing more than nine holes. You want to limit your suffering and the ninth hole puts you back at the clubhouse earlier.

- Pick a time when there are few other players on the course. Marital harmony falters, occasionally, even in the best of marriages. On the golf course make that <u>constantly</u>.

- When playing, <u>never</u> offer advice.

- Praise even the dismal shots. "I know you're in the bunker again, but what a great opportunity to practice".

- By way of distraction, make frequent references to the view, birds, trees, flowers etc; also comments like " We certainly are lucky to be out here on this great summer evening".

- Try to ensure that your spouse knows at least one of your golfing partners fairly well so that conversation can focus on something else besides golf.

- Be obsequious, fawning, and solicitous. Help find lost balls, carry golf bag etc.

- Ply your spouse with small gifts before, during and after the round: golf balls, drinks, treats, coordinated outfits etc.

- Totally disregard the normal rules of golf. Improve lies constantly, give unlimited mulligans, throw balls from the rough into the middle of the fairway, don't count penalty strokes for lost balls and double the normal distance for gimme putts.

Expectations

When you embark on your crusade to become a golfer, it is helpful to have some idea of the normal rate of progress to be expected from your considerable investment in time. Once you have assimilated the fundamentals of the game and played your first 5 to 10 rounds, your score for 18 holes is probably somewhere in the 115 to 140 range. Where can you expect to go from here?

There is some consensus among seasoned golfers that, while learning is fun, achieving a moderate level of competence requires playing about 100 rounds over no more than five years. (My own experience suggests that this estimate is very close.) This means that most of your drives are on the fairway, most of your shots land about where you want them to and you rarely three putt (although your bunker shots and chipping may still need a lot of work). At this level you will be playing bogie or double bogie golf i.e., one or two strokes over par on most holes, with occasional flashes of brilliance and ineptitude. At this stage you will be breaking 100 for 18 holes regularly and can assume to have successfully survived the metamorphosis from a beginner (or duffer) into a golfer. Remember that only about 15 percent of those who play golf and score honestly ever break 100!

Real progress is predicated first, on having sound fundamentals in technique (grip, stance and swing) and second, on the frequency of play. If you haven't acquired these technical basics, your game will probably retain its hit-and-miss nature regardless of how much you play. However, once you have the fundamentals, your ability will depend on how often you play. Your personal goals should be set in direct proportion to the number of times you actually want to play. Work and family responsibilities both compete with golf, undoubtedly the main reasons why most golfers are middle-aged with grown up children and more freedom at work.

The seriousness of your approach to golf can be assessed, in large part, by the reference time frame you use. If you are thinking in terms of games per season you are probably less committed than if you are attempting to play a given number of times per week. To start, I recommend that you try to play no less than 10 to 20 times per season. This means playing almost every week. Having a regular commitment with a foursome at the same time every week or two will help you maintain this pace. Although onerous at first, once you have adjusted to this approach, you can up the rate of play to two or three times per week. As with most other learning experiences, you will find that the more you play, the faster you improve and the more you'll enjoy it.

In terms of progress goals for the beginner, I believe that trying to reduce your average score for 18 holes by 5 strokes per year is realistic. It is more difficult to improve at this rate once you are close to 100 without increasing your frequency of play to an average of twice per week. This worked for me once I was able to play 18 holes each on Saturday and Sunday mornings and 9 holes after work on Wednesdays. Only then, in my 5th year of golf, was I able to regularly break 100.

As your game progresses, you will notice that your score improves in significant increments, not gradually over time. All of a sudden you will improve your game by 5 strokes without any apparent explanation, forgetting for a moment the frustrating rounds and the considerable amount of time spent in practice. The downside is that your game also deteriorates in the same sizable increments when you have been unable to play for some time.

Pre-Season Fitness

A s will become painfully apparent after your first spring session on a driving range or your first few outdoor rounds, golf has a very definite physical dimension. Although your arms and shoulders may be sore, golf is particularly hard on the back. Therefore, it is important to get into some semblance of physical shape before the start of the golf season. Exercise is particularly important for those of us who hibernate during the winter or who assume the role of "couch potato" after hanging up the clubs come fall. Check with your local pro or a fitness club about getting in shape for the season; better still, enroll in a winter golf school to improve your game while maintaining your golfing fitness.

Chapter 5:
Preparing to play

Choosing the Tee-off Time

Now you've decided that you're ready to tackle the golf course and make your "duffer's debut". Remember however, that unlike a traditional "coming out", this is more apt to be a "going in" ... to the rough, the bush and the water, that is. The first thing you must do is book a tee-off time and this as soon as possible, even before you know who you're playing with. The shortest round will take about four hours beyond the time it takes to travel to the course, get ready to play, have a drink, change and return home. It is unlikely that the entire exercise will take less than six hours - a large chunk out of one's day. Both because of the time involved and the fact that golf is a group sport, a definite tee-off time must be arranged with the pro-shop. When making this booking you are usually required to accept a specific time and sometimes to give the names of the other three players. For some strange reason, before the make-up of the foursome is confirmed at tee-off, the names of Tom Smith, Dick Jones and Harry Brown frequently appear on the booking sheet.

The normal way to organize a game is to first confirm that at least one other person is interested in playing at about the same time - say on Saturday morning before 9:00am. Once you have set the time, it is usually easy to complete the foursome. Generally, tee times are only "bookable" two days to a week in advance (except in the case of a tournament) and you'll probably have to give your credit card number to guarantee the booking. It is therefore important to book as early as possible in the morning the required number of days before the planned game. Usually, the chore of booking the time (Tell the greenest member of your foursome that it's an honour.) is shared among the members of a regular foursome, with the booker responsible for advising the other players. One advantage to inheriting the role of the booker is that you have some control over the start time. If, for example, you are not blessed with the metabolism of a fish or a farmer, as a "non-morning" person you might chose to acknowledge your biological clock and postpone the tee-off time as much as possible, while still keeping it within the acceptable timeframe. Given the normal time pressures that affect everyone on weekends, you are apt to find that Saturday morning is the only acceptable option. Afternoon golf is not as popular with spouses (unless you're playing with them) who, while enjoying their morning leisure, also expect a large measure of domestic duty and penance in return for your fun and frivolity on the golf course.

If you are not a morning person but, through force of circumstances hit the links at 6:30am, you may be courting disaster. I find that I can handle mornings as long as I'm not playing at the crack of dawn. If I play really early I can add 5 to 10 strokes to my normal score for 18 holes. If I have carte blanche when selecting a tee-off time, I prefer to play after a large lunch at about 2:00pm. Oddly enough, I have found that playing in the afternoon gives me my best scores. Maybe this is why best ball tournaments usually start after lunch. I am convinced that some people avoid golf because they think it's an early morning game. Regardless of your tee-off time, plan to be there early, and if you are unable to make it on time, give the pro shop as much notice as possible. This allows them the maximum flexibility to reschedule foursomes (including yours) and accommodate other players.

Remember that you are not obliged to make up a foursome in order to play. You can book a time and show up as a single, a twosome or a threesome. Keep in mind that the proshop will try to send golfers off in foursomes, so if you are going it alone, you are likely to be teamed up with better golfers. This is a great opportunity to meet new people and (having introduced yourself as a new golfer), to prove that you will not detract from their game because you are by now fully conversant with golf's customs and conventions.

Using Power Carts

When you book your tee-off time, you will be asked if you need a cart or carts - meaning a power cart (as opposed to a two-wheel pull cart). At vacation area courses renting a cart is often mandatory. This is a major source of revenue and enables the club to process the optimum number of golfers through the course over the day. At regular urban courses, you will have the option: to cart or not to cart? - that is the question.

For most golfers fresh air, moderate exercise and natural scenery are the great attractions of the game. The issue of whether to take a cart does not arise for them, two exceptions being on very hot days and in tournaments, where they can add to the fun. For players with disabilities they are essential. The vast majority of golfers I know seldom use carts. One reason may be that, on those rare occasions when you do have a frustrating round, you are at least able to console yourself with the thought that you have benefited from the fresh air and exercise. Also, seasoned golfers believe that walking actually improves their game by contributing to its rhythm and by allowing them to visualize the next shot as they walk up to their ball.

It is one of life's mysteries that some upscale golf courses continue to offer only the older style gasoline powered carts with their attendant noise and fumes. Given that the typical urban golfer is hoping to escape city sounds and pollution, there is no question that electric carts are a great improvement.

When you decide to take a power cart, remember to respect the rules for their use. Follow the direction signs for carts, particularly near the green and drive according to the rules posted for the day. This usually means: <u>dry days</u> - go anywhere on the fairway; <u>damp days</u> - stay on the cartpath until adjacent to ball and go to and from it at 90 degrees; and, <u>wet days</u> - stay on the cartpath.

Dress Code

The dress code for golf is almost universal, meaning a golf shirt and slacks for men (actually, in golf it's gentlemen). Shirts without sleeves or collars and jeans are not acceptable. If you prefer shorts, be aware that most courses will require them to be knee-length. Some even insist on longer Bermuda-style shorts and knee socks, although most permit sockettes. When trying a new course, I recommend going with the golf shirt and slacks. You will be playing it safe and have fewer problems with bugs and scratchy twigs or nettles as you slash through the rough.

"No"   "Yes"

For ladies, the dress code is slightly more complicated. Jeans are still out but skirts, skorts, golf-length shorts, and slacks are usually in. Tops must have sleeves or a collar but not necessarily both. Sockettes are particularly popular with women. The key to appreciating the dress code for golf is to remember that golf is considered to be a sport for ladies and gentlemen. Think smart/casual or preppy. By the way, don't forget to bring along a change of clothing for after the round, whatever the weather.

Sign-in at the pro shop

You should arrive at the course 45 minutes to one hour before your tee-off time. This gives you time to sign in at the pro shop, change and warm-up by practising your drives, fairway shots, pitching and putting before teeing off. I have found that "the earlier the better" holds true in terms of being entirely ready to play, except when you have a very early tee-off where simply being awake has a very definite advantage over just being physically present.

Your first stop at the course should be at the pro shop to sign in and pay your green fees. This confirms to the pro that your group is a "show" and can be counted on to be on the tee at the scheduled time.

The pro will also let you know if the other members of your foursome have arrived and where they are. When you check in you should therefore tell the pro what your own plans are (e.g. "I'm going for a coffee and then to the driving range" or "I'll be on the putting green.") It is important to remember to keep the pro shop briefed on your plans before you tee off. They will then ensure that the other players in your group are informed of who has shown up and their location. The pro shop's main goal is to help you have an enjoyable day. They value your business and want you back.

Note that at some courses, the pro shop has a starter at the first tee to coordinate the tee-offs. The usual practice is to report to the starter ten minutes before tee-off and then wait on the putting green for your foursome to be called. "Smith, Jones, Brown and Dudley are now on the tee. White, Black, Green and Dolly are on deck."

Last minute checks

Before venturing out onto the range or the course, you will want to get yourself and your equipment ready to play. Think of the Boy Scout motto " Be Prepared". Although this routine may seem like overkill, as you get used to it, it becomes automatic.

The Golfer

Your first thoughts should be to your dress. Will you be warm or cool enough? Do you have a sweater or jacket? Are your golf shoes dry and are the laces and cleats OK? Will you need a rain suit? Do you have a hat? Is your golf glove OK or should you buy a new one? Should you put on sunscreen or insect repellent? Will you need sunglasses? Is there any medication you should bring along? Are you awake?

The Equipment

Next, you should check your equipment.

- Do you have <u>all</u> your clubs? (It's surprising how often you can forget a club during a round. Also remember the maximum number allowed is 14).

- Do you have your umbrella and ball retriever?

- Most importantly - do you have enough balls to get you through the round? For a beginner a worst-case scenario will require as many as a dozen balls for each nine. (In an emergency you can usually restock at the pro shop after the first nine.)

- Do you have tees, ball markers and a pitchfork for repairing ball marks on the greens?

- Do you have a score card and pencil?

Finally, you should decide whether you need a pull-cart or want to carry your clubs. Some golfers consider it "cool" by to carry their clubs. This means less walking around the course but I have found it an aggravation to be continually hoisting the bag onto the shoulders and putting it down. I also prefer a roomy (read: heavier) bag with enough room for all the paraphernalia I need for a trouble-free (not score-wise) round. It is helpful, I believe, for a beginner to look at the entire assortment of clubs before selecting the perfect instrument to play the next brilliant shot. This is easier with a large and upright bag. Although the newer, lighter carry-bags have legs to keep the bag upright, I have found that pulling a cart is less tiring for a duffer who needs to conserve energy so as to make far more shots than the seasoned golfer. My recommendation for beginners is to start out by taking a pull-cart.

Stretching

To the uninitiated, golf appears to place few demands on the body. This is true when you only consider the walking part of the game. Golf works out not only the wrists and shoulders but is also extremely stressful on the lower back and mid-torso. A proper, complete swing requires a full rotation of the upper body around the hips. Unless you are very young, a cold (and/or old) body cannot do this without a warm-up to loosen up your lower back muscles. There are many appropriate warm-up exercises for golf but what is most important is that you actually do them. It only takes two to three minutes but a warm-up will make a marked difference in your game. Having tried the full spectrum of exercises and also having had my share of back problems, I find that a dozen or so practice swings followed by a simple stretching exercise works best and significantly improves flexibility. I rotate first in the direction of the backswing and hold this extreme rotated position for just over a minute and then repeat the exercise for the opposite follow-through position facing forward. It is, apparently, extremely important to hold each stretched position for a full minute.

Pre-game practice

If you intend to give yourself a chance to play your best round, you should, as a beginner, devote a full half hour to your pre-game practice. This allows 20 minutes on the driving range and 10 minutes for chipping and putting. For beginners, the time on the driving range is critical to reinforcing the feeling of a correct swing and to confirm the magnitude of today's slice or hook. A time-tested golf theorem is that it takes 20 practice shots to get your swing into the groove. The choice, of course, is whether to take these practice shots on the range or on the first three or four holes. Presumably, as an eager and enlightened beginner, you will chose the former option where you won't have to count the extra wasted strokes. If you can leave work early during the week to play, you will find frequent opportunities to test this theorem. After fighting your way through city traffic and prying your tensed fingers away from their death grip on the steering wheel, having arrived at the course a mere five minutes before tee-off, you have no time left to relax or practice. My experience in this situation is that the first two holes are an absolute disaster and consequently any hope of achieving a decent score for the first nine is shattered.

Drawing from that font of limitless wisdom, advice and instruction received from pros and seasoned golfers over the years, I follow a practice routine which I have found to be extremely helpful. I take a basket of 30 balls and start by hitting five off the grass with my pitching wedge. I then hit three balls each with my 9, 7, 5 and 3 irons plus my 3 wood. I then hit five balls off a tee with the driver and finish up by hitting the last five with the pitching wedge. I was told by my mentors that the first five shots with the pitching wedge help you to loosen up and get the right smooth tempo for your swing before hitting with the other irons. The last five shots allow you to work on accuracy once you are warmed up. It is important to not hit too many balls on the range before a game. A comment frequently heard is "save some good shots for the course".

It is important for beginners to keep in mind the objective of this pre-game practice - to loosen up and get the feeling of the swing. The less frequently you play, the more important is the practice. Your focus should be on form, consistency and hitting the ball straight. Choice of club (not swing power, which is supposed to be constant) will determine the distance of the shot. Remember, this is not the time to try out new techniques or change your swing!

Once you have finished at the range, move to the practice putting green. While keeping an eye on the time, take out three balls and practice your putting beginning with short three foot putts and then progressing to the longer ten and twenty footers. Your focus should be on distance rather than direction, so that a missed putt will put you no more than a foot or two from the hole. It is difficult for beginners to read the break in greens, but using the right putting weight to roll the ball close to the hole and 12 to 18 inches past it will compensate for this handicap. Since balls from different manufacturers have a slightly different feel, you will find that using the same kind for the 3 you choose for practice will improve your putting more quickly.

In chipping practice you are trying to get the ball airborne to land on the green and then roll to the hole. Start from a single point and try to chip your three balls to different pins on the practice green. Avoid using range balls. These are generally tired and less elastic and won't have the same feel as your own.

Remember that chipping and putting will make up over 50 percent of your shots and should therefore be a major part of your practice! And if you only have 10 minutes before tee-off, rather than rushing to the range, focus on chipping and putting for your entire practice.

By now you should be hearing the starter call out the names of your foursome as either "on deck" or "on the tee". Stop practising and get ready. If you are "on deck", stand well back from the preceding group (20 to 30 yards) and stay quiet until the last player has hit away.

Part C

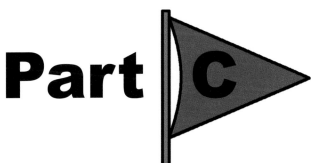

Your Debut - First Time on the Course

Chapter 6:
Scene I - The Tee

As your foursome walks up to the tee, all players should place their pull-carts or bags beside the tee (never <u>on</u> the tee!) where they will be directly en route to the position of their first drive in the fairway. Leaving clubs behind the tee will mean retraced steps and a slower round.

The tee is the launching pad, centre stage, home plate with 3 balls, 2 strikes, 2 out and the bases loaded: the ultimate moment of truth. Before hitting, you should make a few checks. First, your pockets. Do you have two golf balls to start? A spare should be ready when you lose the first one. Are the balls clean (Clean ones are much easier to find.)? You'll also need to have handy: 2 or 3 ball markers, 5 or 6 tees and a pitchfork. Now glance at the hole marker. This gives the number of the hole and the yardage from each set of tee blocks, information vital to helping you select the club you'll use to tee-off.

The first decision for your foursome is, which tee blocks to play from? Traditionally women play from the reds and men from the whites. (If your macho nature tempts you to try the blues, which are considerably more difficult, wait until you've broken par from the whites.) Now you decide who shoots first. Normal procedure is for one player to throw a tee in the air and let it land pointing towards the player who will tee off first. This ritual is then repeated until all players have their tee-off order. If your group is playing from more than one tee, those using the tees farthest from the green shoot first.

The next decision for your group to make is when it's OK to hit. The group in front should be safely beyond the <u>furthest</u> drive of anyone in your group. This probably means no less than 280 to 300 yards. If in doubt, wait! And while waiting, let the shortest hitters (we're talking distance, not stature) go first. A flying ball can maim or even kill if it hits someone in the wrong place.

If you are not the first in your group to tee off, do not choose this moment to practice your swing or chat with other players. You should stand facing or slightly behind the player driving off and at least 15 to 20 feet away. This ensures that you are in a safe zone and well outside the driver's personal hitting space . You should also remain absolutely quiet. Your focus, as a spectator, should be concentrated on where the other golfers' drives land so that any balls going into the rough can be easily found.

Now it's your turn to step up to the tee. If you find yourself nervous, this is perfectly normal and beneficial. Nevertheless, try to be relaxed and stay focused. Choose a flat and relatively undisturbed spot to tee up your ball. The position of the ball on the tee must be from even with the two tee blocks to behind them by not more than two club lengths. With the ball sitting on the cup of the tee which, in turn, is held between your first two fingers, you push down on the ball with your thumb to force the tee into the ground. When your fingers (cradling the tee and the ball) touch the ground, the ball is at the right height. Now rotate the ball so that its logo is at the back where it can be used as an aiming point. Check to ensure that your ball is not in front of the imaginary line between the two tee blocks. Remove any divots, tufts of dead grass or old tees close to your ball to eliminate distractions. Step back until the face of your club is one foot from the ball and take one or two practice swings to loosen up and confirm your technique. Then step forward to address the ball politely. This means getting a proper grip on the club, placing your feet the right distance from the ball and at a 90° angle to your target, taking your stance with the ball at the correct forward-back position between your feet. Using the driver, the ball is generally in line with the inside of the heel of the foot closest to the hole.

Now you are ready to go through your pre-shot routine. Some people waggle their club and cock their head backward or make weird movements while they concentrate on their swing and focus on the ball. The purpose of this routine is to reduce tension while you do the mental and physical preparation for the swing. Each golfer has a slightly different approach. What is important is that the routine be automatic and consistent (And prompt! i.e. it can be extremely frustrating to watch someone dilly-dally over a shot.) My system is to count to five while I go through a quick mental checklist. First I look behind then down the fairway to confirm that all is clear. I then focus on the centre of the logo on the back of the ball, reminding myself to keep my head down and still, and ensuring that my weight is evenly balanced over the balls of both feet. Keeping my eyes locked on the ball, I make the swing and follow through. Then I pray. If at any time while addressing the ball, it falls off the tee or there is a major distraction, step away from the ball for a few seconds and start all over again.

Only after the swing is completed should you take your eyes off the ball and look up to follow its flight and see it landing. (Shout "FORE" as loudly as you can if the ball heads toward someone on an adjoining fairway.) As it lands and rolls to a stop, pick out reference points (a tree, a shrub or a rock) to mark its location. Then step off the tee to let the next player hit. If the ball looks lost, note that you will have to hit a provisional, counting 3 strokes off the tee. Unless you're the last to hit, don't hit the provisional right away. Allow yourself time to relax and refocus before attempting a second tee shot. There is a common and very civilized custom (<u>not</u> in the Rules of Golf) that allows a "Mulligan" or second shot without penalty on the first hole when the first shot is lost or very short. Some unscrupulous players have even been known to take a Mulligan after the first hole or (Yes, it's shocking but true!) more than one Mulligan per round.

Chapter 7:
Scene II - The Fairway

Now that the pressure of the first tee-off is behind you, it's time to enjoy the game. After collecting their clubs, your foursome should walk briskly (stride - don't stroll!) up to the ball that is closest to the tee-off and furthest from the hole. If the ball has become temporarily misplaced, the other players, especially the one with the next closest ball, should help look for it after they have spotted their own balls. Once found, the other players can then proceed to their balls and remain in position, providing they are not in danger of being hit by the shot. Otherwise, they will have to find a safe location until the first player hits. At this point each player should be planning the next shot and selecting the right club in order to save time. When the first player hits, the third and fourth players should spot the shot while the next player to hit walks up to the ball.

If a ball seems to be lost, all players should take no longer than a couple of minutes to carefully beat the bushes looking for it. If the ball was carefully spotted, it should be relatively easy to find; however, after two minutes searching , it is time to carry on. (The Rules of Golf allow five minutes but this option is only exercised in tournament play.) If a ball proves elusive, its owner can then drop a new ball on the fairway opposite to where the lost ball came to rest and count <u>two</u> strokes. This convention is not actually a rule of golf, (It is never seen in competition or tournaments!) but is a good expedient for moving the game along. You are supposed to return to the tee and hit a provisional ball, counting three strokes off the tee. This would generally put your second drive about the same distance from the tee as the first, only this one will be playable while still lying 3. By using this lost ball convention, you are effectively counting the same number of strokes but saving the time it takes to return to the tee. This convention only applies when you are unable to find a ball that you did not consider lost. If your ball is judged to be definitely in golf ball heaven after hitting it from the tee, you should then take a penalty stroke and hit a provisional ball.

Fairways are generously endowed with two officially recognized kinds of hazard - bunkers and water, ignoring the rough - long grass, trees or bush. A beginner's thoughts amid such challenges should turn to the following:

Bunkers: Technique is everything here and should be gleaned from a pro and practised faithfully long before you hit (or try to hit) the course. Your exit strategy (should your ball find its way into a bunker adjacent to the green, where most are located) should include:

- Taking lots of sand with the ball

- Hitting just to get out and not trying for distance

- Making and finishing a full swing

Unfortunately you can't touch the ground with your club in a hazard. Also, don't forget to carefully rake the footprints and other marks in the sand before carrying on.

Water: Unfortunately, the distinctive "plunk" of someone else's ball (yours, that is) hitting the water can become an opportunity to entertain your playing partners. "Friends" in a foursome have been known to offer sympathetic comments like "got your scuba gear?" or "You'll need your rain suit to play that one". Such banter does little to temper your frustration. Now's the time to swallow hard and recover your natural composure. First, after discounting the possibility of encountering alligators or water snakes, see if the ball can be recovered with a ball retriever. (This is a telescopic pole not a dog.) If so, it's important to keep your balance while stretching for the ball. Fall in and your fellow players are sure to erupt in hilarity, do absolutely nothing to help you out, then regale you with fresh perspectives on your plight throughout the round and for months afterward.

Once you have retrieved your ball or taken out a new one, you want to give yourself a decent chance at not repeating the same marine disaster. Find a reasonably flat spot in line with the path of the previous errant shot and back from the red or yellow stakes marking the limits of the hazard, drop your ball, counting <u>one</u> penalty stroke and try again. Should you be so unlucky as to hit the water again, completely ignore the official Rules of Golf (unless you're in a tournament) and immediately walk to the other side of the water and drop again, counting another penalty stroke. Do not, repeat, <u>do not</u> try to continue hitting across the water after losing two balls in the same hazard. By now, you'll be approaching the maximum 10 strokes for the hole and should consider picking up your ball.

Rough: Aptly named, this is a place where you really don't want to be. It usually consists of grass cut longer than the fairway (the first cut) that may become longer (the second cut) the further you get from the fairway. Beyond the verge you may find trees, brush, fallen branches, rocks and - horrors! - creepy crawlies. Before wading in to search for your ball, remember where you are. If it is poisonous snake country, you'll want to rethink the relative importance of the cost of a ball compared to your own survival. A careful look at the foliage will also reveal if you're about to step into poison ivy. Thorns, stinging nettles and animal burrows also await the unwary. Hence my earlier recommendation to wear long pants.

Assuming you have found the ball, carefully examine its lie. If it's near a rock or your swing is in any way interfered with by a tree or branch, don't risk breaking your club thus creating another misguided projectile. There is an easy solution. Loudly declare an "unplayable lie" and move the ball up to two club lengths to a position where the swing can be safely made. You should count a penalty stroke; however, remember that you're a beginner and the objectives are not only to play according to the rules but to have fun, hopefully improve your game, and definitely to survive the round!

Let's assume that your ball is now back in the centre of the fairway and you're ready to make that final approach shot to the green. Since your ball is still furthest from the hole, your companions expect you to proceed. Before stepping up, look for a fairway distance marker. (These may be small shrubs at each side of the fairway at 150 yards, concrete markers in the centre of the fairway at 200, 150 and 100 yards or sprinkler-head covers with the distance marked to the centre of the green.) You then glance at the pin (the pole with the flag indicating the location of the hole) to confirm its position before selecting the right club. Some clubs use pin markers. If the marker on the pin is high, the pin's at the back of the green - low means at the front. Other courses use colour-coded flags with three different colours indicating front, centre or back of the green. Now examine the lie of your ball. If it's in water or on ground under repair on the fairway, as is common in the Spring under "winter conditions," you move it to the side to a normal lie (a "preferred lie") but no closer to the hole. Otherwise your preferred lie becomes a preferred fib. If it's in a divot , move it onto the turf, unless you're in a tournament or determined to practice divot shots, not a good idea for beginners. Then, addressing the ball, you issue the necessary cautions to players with too much confidence in the probable trajectory of your ball, and take a final look at your target before hitting away. Restraining any animal urge to utter a cry of triumph should your shot be close to the pin, the appropriate finale to hitting an iron shot is, of course, to retrieve and <u>replace your divot</u>!

Chapter 8:
Scene III - The Approach

S imilar to courting, greens are not attacked but seduced. Here you must be taciturn, intelligent and crafty, using all the wiles in your inventory. Because you are a beginner, on a typical par 4 hole, your second shot is unlikely to make it onto the green. So, in addition to your drive and fairway iron shot, you'll have to make an approach shot from within 100 yards. This is where the beginner is most vulnerable, since approach shots require the most experience and feel. Whereas the experienced golfer generally puts an approach shot to the green relatively close to the pin, the beginner frequently wastes one or two shots in covering this last 100 yards. The only answer to this dilemma? - practice, practice, practice!

In any case, here are some of the thoughts which should cross your mind as you gain experience making the approach shot to the green:

- Which way is the wind blowing? If there's a smoker in your group, you have a mobile wind guage. Will it cause the ball to drift short or long, to the left or right of the pin? How strong is the wind and will it move the ball 10 or 20 yards?

- Is the elevation of the green above or below my ball? If the green is higher, you may need more club (i.e., a 7 instead of an 8); if lower, less club (a 9 instead of an 8) should be considered.

- Which way does the green slope? After landing, the ball will roll in the direction of the slope. Its steepness will determine how much you have to aim your shot uphill of the pin. (complicated, isn't it?)

- Where is the trouble spot I most want to avoid? If there are bunkers in front or behind the pin on the left of the green while the right side furthest from the pin is clear, aim for the right.

- Is it better to be too long or too short? If the back of the green features bush or heavy rough, plan on playing your ball short.

- Does my lie affect the choice of club? If your ball is on a downhill slope and you want to maintain the usual trajectory of the shot, you will need a more lofted club (an 8 or 9 instead of a 7) to get the same distance as a level shot.

- Can I make the required shot? If the percentages of success are only 1 in 10, forget it and play a safe shot you'll probably make.

If the foregoing leaves you in total despair and intimidated, just aim for the pin and pray. Remember that the vast majority of approach shots fall short of the pin since most golfers (yes, even the really good ones) visualize their ideal rather than usual shot.

Chapter 9:
Scene IV - The Green

As you walk up the fairway, you'll come to see that you're "on the dance floor", close to pin-high, and that it's time to finish off the hole. As a beginner you will likely feel a sense of relief at having finally reached the green. Here your chances increase to perform as well as any seasoned golfer. From a beginner's perspective, effective putting requires far less experience and disciplined technique than the wood or iron shots, and on this level playing field you have a chance to show your stuff. But before you become too euphoric, get your brain in gear: it's time to plan the next move.

Walking up to the green, you must first decide where to leave your pull-cart or bag. Many beginners make the mistake of leaving their clubs where they made the last approach shot. This move is definitely a time waster and a move sure to label you as the "duffer" you are. It is also unsafe, since you are putting yourself in the line of fire from the group following yours. The right thing to do is to take your clubs to a spot just off and behind the green and en route to the next tee. You are never to pull your cart on the green. Try to keep it at least 1 to 2 yards away from the green to reduce wear and tear on this high-traffic area, thereby helping to keep the turf in good condition for those difficult short chip shots.

The first order of business before putting, is using your pitch-fork, to repair the ball mark left by your approach shot. While they are at it, experienced golfers usually repair any other ballmarks they see.

The rules of golf require the player whose ball is farthest from the hole to shoot first, whether it is on the green or not. The convention followed by most golfers requires everyone to be on the green before this rule is applied to putting. Regardless, once you are on the green and have deposited your clubs, you must mark your ball. Walk up to the ball and, being careful not to step on the line between any ball and the hole, place a marker behind the ball and in line with the side away from the hole and pick up your ball. Wipe it off with the palm of your hand or a towel and step back to plan your putt while those farthest from the hole proceed in turn. If your ball is closest to the hole, you should hold the pin for the players with longer putts so they can see the target or remove the pin if they want. Remember, a putted ball hitting the pin is a 2 stroke penalty.

While waiting and planning your putt, look carefully at the line of the putt, its uphill or downhill slope, and its break. Is the slope slight or steep? Is it left to right or right to left? Will it be a two-inch break, a six-inch, or straight in? Here you can get some great feedback from watching other putts; these will also tell you if the green is fast or slow.

Now that it's your turn, step smartly up to your marker, reposition your ball in front of it, and then remove the marker. When addressing the ball (with deference and respect; you are, after all, a mere beginner) confirm your line and estimate the weight of the putt. Here it is also a good idea to take a practice swing and pick an aiming point, such as a spot on the green or a mark on the cup, before hitting away. If you sink the putt, retrieve it promptly (again, carefully avoid other putt lines) and step out of the way. If your putt has rolled to within 1-1/2 to 2 feet of the hole, you look pleadingly at your fellow players (who may occasionally and inexplicably be stricken with lockjaw) in the hope of being awarded a "gimme". This concession, not in the Rules of Golf, allows you to pick up your ball without putting it but still counting one stroke. As long as your foursome is keeping pace, as a beginner you should try even the gimme putts to get the practice. If your putt is the first into the hole, proceed to the pin and be ready to pick it up and replace it as soon as the last putt goes in. Now, your group can pick up their clubs and proceed to the next hole. As you're walking over, the scorekeeper will usually ask for your scores - the normal question (very appropriate for beginners) being "What's the damage?"

Based on these scores, you will have established the "honour" or tee-off order for the next hole (i.e., the player with the lowest score tees off first). You are now ready to carry on with the next hole and continue your round. Award yourself an "attaboy" or "attagirl" ("attaperson" is not used in golf) if, despite having thrashed your score into the double digits, you have observed all the required courtesies and conventions.

Chapter 10:
Managing the Round

A typical round of 18 holes takes about 4 hours to play - a bit of a rush for beginners. This allows 2 hours for each 9 holes, 40 minutes for every 3 holes, or an average of 13 minutes for each hole, giving you about 10 minutes to play each hole and 3 minutes to proceed to the next tee and get ready. From the beginner's perspective, shooting 120 for an 18 hole round, means 180 minutes of active playing time and an average of 1-1/2 minutes for each shot (including walking and planning). Contrast this pace with that of an experienced (and relaxed) golfer shooting 80 who has 2-1/4 minutes for each stroke or 50% more time! And, if the seasoned golfer were to move at the same pace as the beginner, the 18 holes would take about 171 minutes (80 x 1.5 + 17 x 3) or 2 hours and 51 minutes. No wonder beginners have that stressed and harried look when trying to play a round in the "normal" time. This calculation also shows why time spent on the driving range is such a good investment! Remember that an enjoyable, low-score round has its own steady rhythm and regular intervals between shots. This rhythm is preserved by maintaining a steady (i.e., undelayed) pace of play.

In addition to the time taken to play the game, there are other considerations which may affect the time to complete a round:

- **Washroom stops** - There are usually washrooms at the half and quarter way points, with the half-way house (usually near the clubhouse) having the best facilities. Remember that a round of golf is a four hour commitment, so don't fill up on liquids before venturing out!

- **Lunch / snack break** - This interlude can last no longer than 5 minutes and may be taken at the halfway point, as long as play is not held up. Order up your sandwich and drink and carry them with you. Remember to keep up to the group in front.

- **Lost clubs** - This can really delay your game, particularly if you decide to try to find the missing club immediately. Instead of starting on a wild goose chase, continue play with a substitute. Invariably the group behind you will pick up your club and return it. If you happen to find a club, stick it in your bag and, at your earliest opportunity, hail the group in front. If it's not one of theirs, return it to the pro shop after the round. Golfers are really an honest lot, and no-one wants your old clubs anyway. One way to ensure the prompt return of lost clubs is to mark them individually with your name and telephone number.

- **The pressure of following players -** Beginners tend to be extremely aware of the group playing behind them and worry about holding up their play. For some this is such an obsession that they are unable to concentrate on their own game, often with disastrous consequences. Try to focus on your own play and, unless you lose a ball, don't worry about the following group until you have finished the hole.

- **Slow play in front** - Considerate players should let you play through (i.e., pass them) if they're holding you up. If the offer is not made, speak to the course marshal about the problem. If the marshal is not around, choose an opportune moment to politely and tactfully ask the group in front if they would mind letting you play through sometime over the next several holes.

- **If one or more holes are open in front**, speed up your play! You have an obligation to stay up to the group in front. If you are unable to do this, let the group behind play through.

- **If the group behind hits up to you**, remember, there is no excuse for endangering other players. A golf ball striking a vulnerable spot can cause a serious injury, even kill. If you encounter this situation, assume it is an accident and speak to the group behind. I have encountered players who hit up to the group in front intentionally to send a message about slow play, but this is totally unacceptable behaviour and should be reported to the marshal or starter as soon as possible. Under no circumstances, do you hit the ball back at the offending players or engage in any other kind of threatening behaviour.

- **Hitting up to the group in front** - Apologize at the earliest opportunity and don't do it again!

- **Scoring -** Reporting one's score among better players can be an intimidating exercise for beginners since they might feel ashamed of their high scores. But be aware that all the better players have "been there", can score high on any given hole and have bad days too. I have seen top players hit pitiful shots off the first tee, or worse, whiff on the first tee and score 13 on a hole. Admittedly, they don't do this often, but the fact that it can happen means they are unlikely to be surprised by anything you do or don't do. More importantly, you will come to realize that other players are more interested in their own game than in yours. As long as you play efficiently and respect the conventions and customs of golf, other players will focus on your charming disposition, conversation and sense of humour as opposed to your score. I know several low handicappers who regularly take high handicappers out to golf, not because of their golfing abilities but because they're just "fun to be with".

Chapter 11:
The 19th Hole

Unlike the pros and keeners who practice after they play, you will, as a beginner, find it a supreme relief to relax after sinking that last putt. While savouring this moment, you will want to observe one of golf's most important etiquettes - shaking hands with the other players to thank them for the round. This is usually done after the pin is placed in the hole and prior to leaving the green. Then, as you are walking toward the clubhouse, give your score for the 18th hole to the scorekeeper for your foursome and note the time you've taken to play the round, ideally not more than 4 hours and 10 minutes.

Now you will want to return your pull cart (or electric cart, if you were forced to take one) to the pro-shop and stow your equipment. This wrap-up includes wiping off your golf shoes on the cleaning brushes and stowing your glove in your bag along with golf balls, tees, markers, and pitchfork. The custom of most golfers is to change and wash up . It's also a good idea to shower, especially on a hot day, if facilities are available, as the five-mile walk leaves you drenched.

You can now look forward to the greatest moment in golf - reliving the round over cool, liquid refreshment. As a beginner, you will probably not be inclined to call a press conference to announce your score, but that is irrelevant. During this rehash the focus is, first and foremost, on the good (if not great) shots. In all probability this should entitle you to at least 2 or 3 honourable mentions. Talk will inevitably turn to the unfortunate disasters caused by bad luck, distractions, unfavourable environmental conditions, bad lies, poor pin placements and the dismal condition of the fairways. Strangely, there will be no talk of inexperience, ineptitude, incompetence or stupidity. Thus the great attraction of golf. There are no winners and losers - only participants. The tone of these post-mortems is singular for its forgiveness, generosity and encouragement. The great common bond of golfers, regardless of ability, is the shared view of the game's essential challenge: the player against the course. Rather than a sense of "victor and vanquished", the mood of a foursome is akin to that of soldiers having fought and survived a battle. All players thereby avail themselves of the greatest benefit and most obvious truth of golf: that "there are no losers on the golf course" and "to play is to win".

Part D

Duffer's Do's

Checklists for Beginners

Unlike the official Rules of Golf which set out how the game is to be played, these checklists provide a simple guide for beginners to help them learn golf and adapt to its culture as easily and quickly as possible.

A. Learning the game

The first and most important challenge to be faced by the beginner...and an investment in your future enjoyment of the game.

- Find a friend to learn and play the game with you.

- Buy equipment you like that feels good.

- Take instruction from a certified teaching pro.

- Practice, practice, practice - on a driving range.

- Practice or play not less than once a week during the season.

- Practice all aspects of the game: driving, iron shots, bunker shots, pitching, and putting.

- Don't play on a regular course until you can hit 75 to 80 percent of your shots close to where you aim them.

- Don't play 18 holes until your score for 9 is under 65.

- Play par 3 courses or in best-ball tournaments as much as possible.

- Pick a course you like and stay there.

- Play with people you like.

- Play mostly with people of about the same ability.

- Don't take yourself too seriously; no-one else will.

- Enjoy learning and have fun!

B. Being ready to play

It is important to be ready to play before venturing out onto the course. Since golf is a sport of concentration rather than reaction, it depends on both a relaxed mental focus and physical preparation.

- Book a tee-off time friendly to your biological clock.

- Avoid the earliest times, when the course is fully booked and the pressure for fast play is greatest.

- Arrive at the course an hour before tee-off.

- Check your equipment upon arrival.

- Do some stretching exercises before hitting practice balls.

- Take 30 balls and 20 minutes to warm up on the range.

- Start and end your warm-up with the pitching wedge.

- Adjust your drives for any hook or slice you see in practice.

- Use 3 balls to practice chipping and putting on the practice green.

- Be ready to proceed to 1st tee when called.

C. Playing safely

Golf can be a dangerous sport if basic common sense conventions are ignored. Experienced golfers live in mortal fear of being maimed or mutilated by beginners. Make your day a safe one by observing the following rules:

- Wait to hit until the preceding group is well beyond your <u>longest</u> shot.

- Ensure fellow players are clear before making your swing.

- Shout "FORE" if your ball heads toward other golfers.

- Stand five yards away and parallel to or behind players about to swing.

- Move your ball away from rocky lies.

- When your swing is interfered with by rude trees, bushes, rocks, move the ball.

- Exit each green at the rear to avoid being hit by following players' approach shots.

- When lightning threatens, leave the course immediately.

- In snake/alligator country, stay out of the rough and water hazards.

- Advise following players immediately when they hit up close to your group.

- Wear a hat and sunscreen when playing between 10:00am and 3:00pm.

D. Efficient golf

An enjoyable, low score round has a steady rhythm and regular interval between shots. Unforeseen delays and the frustration of looking for lost balls can interrupt this rhythm and raise your score. To keep the rhythm:

- Aim for a four hour round.

- Stay up to the group in front.

- At the green, put your clubs where you won't have to retrace steps on leaving.

- Allow only two minutes to look for each lost ball.

- When delayed, let the group behind play through.

- When you are able to hit safely, hit away. (Ready Golf)

- When you're not hitting, watch the other players' shots.

- Pick up your ball when your score is 10 on any hole.

- The first player on the green should man the pin and remove it when ready.

- If pressed for time, take "gimmes" for balls 1-1/2 to 2 feet from the hole.

- The first player to finish putting should retrieve the pin and replace it in the hole after the others have holed out.

- Study your putt from <u>one</u> direction only before putting.

- Take lunch "on the fly" and do not stop for more than 5 minutes.

- After all players have finished putting, clear the green immediately.

E. Course Etiquette

Appropriate behaviour is very much a part of golf. The following courtesies respect the protocol and traditions of the game and are unfailingly observed by mature and responsible players:

- Respect the order of play unless the player away is not ready.

- Keep quiet when other players are addressing the ball and shooting.

- Respect the comfort zone of players hitting - 5 to 10 yards.

- Praise all good shots by other players.

- Stay silent or offer condolences on poor shots by other players.

- Stand facing or slightly behind the player who is hitting.

- Help other players look for their lost balls.

- Replace divots and repair ball marks properly.

- On the green, never walk on the putting lines of other players' balls.

- Stand back so your shadow doesn't fall on other players' putting lines.

- Pick up the wedges set aside by other players busy putting out.

- Return any clubs found on the course to the pro shop.

- After putting out on the final green, thank your fellow players for the round.

F. Low Stress golf

Careless golf is not carefree golf but is actually fraught with frustrations. To keep them within manageable limits, the following precautions are highly recommended:

- Practice on a driving range to bring your game up to course-playing level.

- Arrive at the course a full hour before tee-off.

- Stretch and warm up before tee-off.

- Take 12 balls with you for each round.

- Never look for a lost ball for longer than 2 minutes.

- When a ball is definitely lost, forget it.

- Pick up your ball when your score is 10 on any hole.

- If a particular club is not working during a round, stop using it.

- When a second shot goes into the same water hazard, drop on the far side.

- Enjoy the company, the fresh air and the exercise.

G. Care of the Course

The quality of any golf game is partially determined by the quality of the course. To help preserve this quality, all golfers should, as a matter of "course:"

- Replace or repair all divots on tees and fairways.

- Repair all ball marks (your own and others) on each green.

- Keep pull-carts and bags at least 2 to 3 yards away from the green.

- Keep pull-carts out of the long grass.

- Don't litter.

- Respect all rules for using power carts. Follow directional signs, particularly near the green, and drive the cart according to the rules posted for the day. These are usually: <u>dry days</u> - go anywhere on fairway; <u>damp days</u> - stay on the cartpath until adjacent to the ball and drive to and from it at a 90 degree angle; <u>wet days</u> - stay on the cartpath.

- Lay (don't drop!) clubs or flagstick on the greens.

- Keep off "Ground under Repair".

- Avoid worn spots on the fairway and near greens.

- Rake the disturbed sand in bunkers after hitting out.

H. Profile of an Ideal Beginner

Experienced golfers frequently complain about the behaviour of beginners. Despite a widespread conviction that beginners as a valued species rank somewhere between mosquitoes and poison ivy, the truth is that the thrust of their complaints is directed not at newcomers' golfing ability (or lack of it), so much as at their ignorance of the culture, customs, and conventions of golf. How well beginners play the game as opposed to how well they score is the issue. Those who shoot 130 but make a point of respecting other players, the course, and the game's conventions will find they receive a warm welcome as fellow golfers. Beginners who score lower but do not "play the game" will find themselves tolerated but will seldom be invited to play again.

A wish list of the characteristics golfers would like to see in the ideal beginner would look something like this. They

- Play with an eye to the safety of other golfers.

- Are courteous at all times.

- Respect other players and the course.

- Replace all fairway divots and repair ball marks on the green.

- Do not dally.

- Welcome advice from other players.

- Constantly try to improve their game.

- Keep the ball mostly on the fairway.

- Do not waste time looking for lost balls.

- Maintain composure and sense of humour, often under trying (read embarrasing) circumstances.

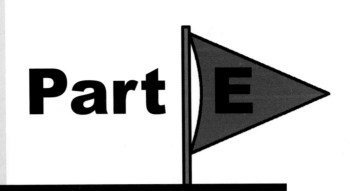

Part E

Epilogue & References

Epilogue

Now that you have thoroughly absorbed the essence of "Duffer's Debut", you have a basic understanding of "what this game is all about." Although this book has, on occasion, referred to technical aspects of golf in order to convey the full dimension on the game, I have deliberately avoided detailed discussions on technique. Not only am I emphatically unqualified to tackle this subject, but my intent has been to focus on the other, nontechnical aspects that have been, over the years, extremely intimidating for newcomers.

Golf has not been kind to those learning the game. The culture and rules are complex and perceived as elitist and bureaucratic. Youngsters are encouraged to take up the game with their parents only to be left to founder as young adults when lack of time and high costs prevent them from continuing until they reach middle age. Despite these drawbacks, the tradition, mystique and other attractions of golf still draw countless beginners to the sport each year.

I therefore sincerely hope that this contribution to your knowledge of the customs, conventions and culture of golf has demystified the sport to some extent and helped forearm you, the humble beginner, with enough of the basics that you will be able to savour, nay relish the great game of golf. A positive perspective will enable you to approach the game with confidence and to experience one of life's great pleasures in the company of your fellow golfers.

As a beginner who believes that golf, like life, is a continuous learning experience, I welcome any feedback which you, the reader, feel would be helpful to fellow novices. E-mail me at "ted@duffersdebut.com"

May your fairways be sunny and warm, your drives long and straight, your irons accurate and your putts short. Most importantly, may your golfing companions be congenial and witty about both your best and worst efforts!!

Glossary of Golfing Terms

Address
the positioning of your body relative to the ball before swinging

Albatross
a score, on a hole, of three shots under par - usually a 2 on a par 5

Away
clear to hit or, it's your turn, as in " you're away"

Bogie
a score, on a hole, of one shot over par i.e., a 5 on a par 4. There is also double bogie meaning two shots over par and triple bogie meaning three shots over par

Birdie
a score on a hole of one shot under par i.e., a 3 on a par 4

Break
the lateral distance a struck ball will roll to the left or right of the hole on a sloping green

Bunker
a sandtrap

Cartpath
the narrow path beside each hole intended for use by power carts. Note that if the path is wide and asphalted, you're probably on a "carpath" or road and could encounter an onrushing Buick!

Casual water
puddles or saturated ground on a part of the course which is normally dry. Relief is taken by moving the ball sideways (no closer to the hole) to just outside the casual

water such that both the ball and your stance are on playable terrain. (Note: there is no "formal" water)

Chip
a relatively short, initially airborne then rolling shot to the green, using a short, lofted iron

Closed faced club
a club held so that its clubface, instead of being in line with the shaft, perpendicular to the direction of the shot, is angled slightly forward toward the green

Cup
the metal container that supports the sides of the hole and holds the flagstick.

Distance markers
shrubs or small trees on either side of the fairway 150 yards from the hole or concrete markers embedded in the centre of the fairway at 200, 150 and 100 yards from the hole or sprinkler head covers (round metal plates) with the distance marked to the centre of the green

Divot
the strip of turf removed by an iron when, after hitting the ball, it strikes the grass - the resultant hole.

Driver
the No. 1 or largest wood used to hit the ball as far as possible from the tee. Because of its long shaft and higher clubhead speed, the driver gives a golfer the longest but also the least accurate shot, due to its relatively low loft. Also the player at the wheel of the powercart.

Draw   a shot whose flight path is a slight curve toward the golfer - to the left for a right-handed golfer.

Duff   to miss-hit a shot

Duffer   a high handicapper who is basically inept or has not yet learned the game. Unlike a hacker, there is hope that a duffer will improve.

Eagle   a score on a hole of two shots under par i.e., a 3 on a par 5 (something a beginner doesn't have to worry about)

Fade   a shot whose flight path is a slight curve away from the golfer - to the right for a right-handed golfer.

Fescue   tall, tough grass planted as rough which conceals and envelops a ball, making it difficult to regain the fairway with any club other than a pitching wedge.

Gimme   a short (1 to 1-1/2 ft.) putt judged to be "unmissable" and therefore conceded by the other player(s). The ball is picked up without the necessity of putting out. Not part of the rules of stroke play golf, gimmes are used by most players (except in tournaments) and are generally given as a courtesy to maintain the pace of play.

Golfer   a player who has an average score of less than 100 for 18 holes.

Grip   the way the hands are placed when holding a club. Also the top part of the club covered in leather or rubber.

Ground under repair   (GUR) an area of the course, usually marked by ropes or lines painted on the turf, which is judged to be unsuitable for play. Relief is taken by moving the ball sideways or laterally (but not closer to the hole) to just outside the GUR .

Hacker   a high handicapper who is all force and no finesse. This is usually a pejorative term which refers more to a player's attitude than their capability. Unlike the dufffer, the hacker views the game as purely a physical challenge without the essential mental dimension.

Handicap   the figure, for a golfer playing a given course, indicating the difference between par and the average score among the best 10 of the golfer's last 20 games.

Hanidcap Index   a golfer's handicap adjusted to take into account the relative difficulty of the courses played using each course's slope rating.

Halfway House   a small shack between the 9th and 10th holes, or part of the main clubhouse where you may get a quick sandwich and drink or find a washroom.

Hazard   a bunker (generally a sandtrap) or watery area (pond, ditch, river, lake, ocean) It does not include the rough.

Honour   the privilege of teeing off first on a hole based on having the best score on the previous hole.

Hook   a shot whose flight path is a sharp curve toward the golfer (to the left for a right-handed golfer)

Hosel   the short hollow section of the clubhead which surrounds the end of the shaft.

Lateral water hazard   water that lies beside or parallel to your route to the hole. It is usually marked by red or yellow stakes.

Lie   the position of your ball in terms of the probability of making solid contact with the ball when you make your swing. If the ball is in a divot hole or buried deep in the grass, it's a "bad lie". If it's sitting up, allowing you to make a normal shot, it's a "good lie" <u>or</u> - the angle between the sole of the clubface and the shaft. Also, a colourfully exaggerated story of how the ball you hit into the bush came to land on the top of a clump of grass with a clear view of the green.

Links   the golf course or an open, treeless type of course, frequently seen in coastal areas.

Loft   the angle of the clubface.

Long irons   2, 3 or 4 irons or those with the longest shafts.

Loose impediments	natural objects such as stones, leaves, twigs, branches and worms on the green or fairway which may be moved without penalty to allow a clear shot at the ball.
Marshal	a member of the pro shop staff responsible for maintaining the pace of play on a course. They usually tour the course in a power cart with a flag on the cart marked "Marshal"
Mid-irons	5, 6, or 7 irons, generally used for fairway approach shots or tee shots on long par 3's
Mulligan	A second shot off the tee when the first dismal effort is duffed, lost or pitifully short. Purists (among those who subscribe to Mulligans) will usually allow this second chance only on the first tee.
Open faced club	a club held so that its clubface, instead of being in line with the shaft, (i.e. perpendicular to the direction of the shot) is pointed slightly backwards, toward the tee. Also, a selection on the lunch menu at the halfway house.
Out of bounds	the area outside the golf course, usually marked by white stakes.
Par	the "ideal" score for a given hole including two putts on the green in addition to the tee shot and approach shot(s).
Pin	the flagstick whose banner often indicates the number of the hole. It also usually has

a marker on the shaft indicating the position of the hole relative to the centre of the green.

Pin-high
a term used to describe a ball which has been hit the right distance and is lying in line with the pin or flag.

Pitch
a relatively short, high, mostly airborne shot with little roll, usually made to the green using a wedge. Also the high tone of voice used by one spouse in response to the other's suggestions to make a particular shot.

Pitchfork
the small fork with two tines used to repair ball marks on the green.

Play through
to pass the preceding group of players due to their slower than normal play.

Power cart
the 4-wheeled vehicle used to transport 2 players around the course.

Preferred lie
where the ball is placed without penalty on flat, level ground, usually when the condition of the fairway is generally poor or inconsistent. This is a common practice just after courses are opened in the spring and 'winter rules' are said to apply. This provision, when posted at the first hole, allows players to use preferred lies.

Pro shop
the store where the head pro and his assistants book tee-off times, arrange lessons and sell golf equipment and clothing.

Provisional a second ball, hit when the first one is judged to be lost.

Pull a shot hit straight but on an angle towards the hitter instead of down the centre of the fairway.

Pull cart a 2-wheeled light cart used to carry a golf bag and its clubs. Most are manual but there are also electric motorized versions.

Push a shot hit straight but on an angle away from the hitter instead of down the centre of the fairway.

Putter the club with a vertical face - used on the green to tap the ball and roll it into the hole.

Ready golf the practice of golfers hitting as soon as the way is clear and they are ready, instead of strictly following the rule of the player farthest from the hole hitting first.

Rough the first cut adjacent to the fairway (known commonly as the <u>short</u> rough) or the uncut grass beyond the first cut (known commonly as the <u>long</u> rough)

Scull to hit the top half of the ball on the swing resulting in a flat, low shot.

Shank to hit the ball sideways off the hosel of the club.

Short irons 8, 9 irons and wedges with the shortest

shafts, generally used for short fairway approach shots or tee shots on short par 3's.

Sky to hit the ball high (usually with the driver and unintentionally) by hitting underneath it.

Slice a shot whose flight path is a sharp curve away from the golfer or to the right for a right-handed golfer.

Slope a number assigned to golf courses which rates their difficulty relative to a baseline standard course rated at 100.

Stance where or how you place your feet

Sweet spot the central area of a clubface which, when striking the ball produces a solid, dead-centre hit.

Swing The body motion when a golfer attempts to hit the ball. Also a music style familiar to most senior golfers.

Tee a cupped wooden peg on which the ball is placed to hit the first shot on each hole. **or** - the raised, grassed mound (known as the teeing ground) on which the ball is placed behind the tee blocks to hit the first shot on a hole.

Tee blocks the pair of coloured (usually red, white or blue) markers on the tee behind which the ball must be placed before hitting.

Unplayable lie	a ball position that prevents you from making a safe swing (or any swing at all). When you declare an unplayable lie, a penalty stroke is taken and the ball may be dropped no closer to the hole than either: two clublengths either from where it came to rest or anywhere back on the line of the shot.
Water hazard	a pond or stream that lies in the way of your route to the hole. It is marked by yellow stakes (and, unfortunately, is usually wet).
Wedges	short irons used for approach shots to the green. These include pitching wedges, sand wedges and lob wedges.
Whiff	a swing that completely misses the ball.
Winter rules	a convention allowing players on winter or weather damaged fairways to move their ball up to one clublength, but no closer to the hole, to a preferred (and presumably normal) lie.

Index

A

albatross 99
annual golf tournament 36
approach 67
assistant pros 33
away 99

B

ball 15—16
ball diameter 15—16
ball retriever 63
being ready to play 84—85
best ball 36, 44
biological clock 44
birdie 99
bogie 40, 99
books 20
break 99
bunker 62, 68, 99
buying equipment 26—31

C

care of the course 92—93
cartpath 99
casual water 99
cavity-backed 29
chip 100
chipping 53
cleaning brushes 79
closed faced club 100
clothing 30
clubs 17—18
computer games 21
cost 6
couch potato 42
course Etiquette 89—90
cup 100
custom made golf shop 28

D

damp days 46
dedication ix
difficulties 14
distance markers 100
divot 65, 100
double bogie 40
draw 16, 101
dress code 47—48
driver 100
driving range 33, 35, 42
dry days 46
duff 36, 101
duffer 36, 40, 50, 101

E

eagle 101
efficient golf 87—88
elevation of the green 68
epilogue 97
equipment 15, 49—53
expectations 39—42

F

fade 16, 101
fairway 5, 13—14, 61
fairway distance marker 65
fescue 101
fitness 42
fore 59—60, 86
foursome 43, 53, 57
fundamentals 41

G

garage sales 28
gimme 73, 88, 101
glossary of golfing terms 99
golf 3
    goal of 9
    What is golf? 3
    When is golf played? 6
    Who plays golf? 3—4
    Why play golf? 7—8
    with spouse 38—39
golf balls 29—30
golf glove 31
golf shoes 28—29
golf store 27
golfer 3, 36, 40, 49, 101
    characteristics: 3
greatest moment in golf 80
green 14—15, 68, 71
green slope 68
ground under repair 102

H

hacker 102
halfway house 102
handicaps 10
hazard 5, 102
hole 39
hole marker 57
home putting greens 22
honour 103
hook 16, 51, 103
hosel 103

I

indoor driving ranges 21
initiation 25—26
introduction xi—xii

L

last minute checks 49—50
lateral water hazard 103
learning the game 83—84
lessons 31—34
lie 64, 68, 103
links 5—6, 103
loft 18, 103
lofted club 68
long irons 103
loose impediments 104
lost clubs 76
low stress golf 90—91

lunch / snack break 76

M

magazines 20
  Golf 20
  Golf Digest 20
marker 72—73
marshal 104
mid-irons 104
Mulligan 60, 104

N

newspaper ads 28

O

off-course golf 19
on deck 53
on the tee 53
open faced club 104
opening time 6
out of bounds 104

P

pace 75
par 9, 104
par 3 course 35
pin 68, 104
pitch 105
pitchfork 31, 57, 105
play through 105
playing safely 85—87
power cart 45, 45—46, 46, 105
  rules 46
pre-game 51
  practice 51—53
pre-shot routine 59
preferred lie 105
pressure of following players 77
pro shop 27, 48, 105
Profile of an Ideal Beginner 93—94
progress goals 41

pros 32, 33, 34
provisional 106
public course 36
pull 106
pull-cart 50, 106
pull-carts 57
push 106
putter 106

R

ready golf 106
rough 64, 68, 106
round 75—76
rounds 39
rules 11—12
  The Rules of Golf 12
  two key rules 11
rules of golf 17—18, 62, 64, 72

S

scoring 78
scramble 36
scull 106
shank 106
short irons 106
sign-in 48
sky 107
slice 16, 51, 107
slope system 10
slow play in front 77
sporting goods store 27—28
stance 107
stretching 50
stroke 40
sweet spot 107

T

technique 41
tee 13, 16—17, 57—60, 107
tee blocks 57, 58, 107
tee times 44
tee-off 43, 43—45, 44, 48, 57, 85

tee-off time 36
tee-offs 48
teeing off 48
television 19—20
topography 5—6
trajectory 17—18
trouble 11—12

U

unplayable lie 108

W

washroom stops 76
water 63—64
water hazard 108
wedges 108
wet days 46
whiff 108
wind 68
winter golf school 34—42, 42
winter rules 108

Y

yardage marker 13

About the Author

Ted Ronberg is not an authority on golf, having spent most of his working life as a management consultant, developing and running adult training programs and translating analyses of complex issues into simple, straightforward language. This skill has now been directed at Ted's considerable experience in learning golf, a sport he has been duffing at for six years. Although he has, in the past, despaired that he was doomed to remain a perpetual beginner, Ted is now convinced that he is on the verge of awakening his true athletic potential and has begun to measure his emerging prowess, not just by the number of balls lost per round, but also by the number of strokes. He feels strongly that there is no sport more difficult to learn for beginners and is amazed that the orientation or non-technical aspect of the game is largely unaddressed by golf writers. As a veteran beginner, Ted has undertaken this challenge in writing - Duffer's Debut - where liberal use of humour complemented by topical cartoons make this a light, interesting and fun introduction to golf.

About the Illustrator

Kieron O'Gorman is an accomplished golf cartoonist and systems engineer who, through his illustrations and cartoons of duffers Dudley and Dolly, has successfully captured the lighter side of golf and the key points of the text. He hopes to one day to elevate his duffing ability to match Ted's.